I will not fear

I will not fear

My Story *of a* Lifetime of Building Faith under Fire

MELBA PATTILLO BEALS

Revell

a division of Baker Publishing Group
Grand Rapids, Michigan

Published by Revell
a division of Baker Publishing Group
PO Box 6287, Grand Rapids, MI 49516-6287
www.revellbooks.com

Printed in the United States of America

Library of Congress Cataloging in Publication Control Number: 2017036626

ISBN 978-0-8007-2943-1

Some names and details have been changed to protect the privacy of the individuals involved.

18 19 20 21 22 23 24   7 6 5 4 3 2 1

To Grandmother, India Annette Peyton,
and Mother, Dr. Lois Maria Pattillo,
who blessed me with the belief in a living God

To my brother, Conrad Pattillo,
who demonstrated by a lifetime of police work his
contribution to social advances, commitment to God,
and honoring right over wrong and good over bad

Contents

Foreword

I Will Not Fear is one of the most inspiring books we have ever read. Dr. Beals's writing is honest and compelling, and it is the kind of book you cannot put down. It should be required reading for every American. She brings to life every story and milestone on her journey in such a way that we cannot help but take it with her. Our deepest gratitude to her for sharing her terrorizing walk so that we have a window into what it means and what it takes to be "a profile in courage."

Melba was blessed with an amazing grandmother, India, who through courageous determination in harrowing circumstances sought medical help for Melba and her mother at her birth. She instilled in Melba, during her first fifteen years of life, that her purpose here on earth was to fulfill God's assignment for her, wherever that would lead her. It has often been said that if a child has just one person who has faith in them, they have a far greater chance of not only surviving but also thriving, regardless of their life circumstances. Melba's grandmother not only had faith in her but also passed on the

9

gift of faith that would guide and sustain her the remaining decades of her life, particularly after Grandmother India's passing. She gave her some of the greatest gifts one could give, including the lifetime gift of the certainty of God's undying love for her and the precious gift of having God as her friend. She opened Melba's terrified young heart to the concepts of gratitude and, ultimately, forgiveness—two of the most important aspects of being a free human being. Her grandmother also instilled in her the belief that God is with her always—and would be through life—to help and guide her through any challenge she would face.

As one of the famous Little Rock Nine who first integrated the all-white Central High School in Little Rock, Arkansas, Melba was not only, quite literally, on the forefront of the desegregation movement in America but on the front pages of the major newspapers as well. She bravely entered the school, guarded by soldiers of the 101st Airborne Division and confronted with raging, violent, white citizens. This would become the testing ground of her faith. Physical and psychological threats, severe bullying, hatred, and bigotry surrounded her on all sides each day, fueled by the Ku Klux Klan's very real, life-threatening influence. And she was only fifteen years old.

There was, and is to this day, a spiritual strength that allowed Melba to return to school each day in an environment filled with dread. The jeering by whites was so vicious and volatile that each moment held the threat of both psychological and physical harm—even death.

God's plan for Melba also included healing her own terror of and prejudice against white people, so as to inspire others to do the same. God gave her the McCabe family, Quakers living in rural Santa Rosa, California. Bless that family's dear hearts, each and every one of them. They helped to heal not only a traumatized girl but also a divided nation.

We have known Melba for many decades and have shared each other's journeys. She has an amazing charisma and is filled with power, kindness, gentleness, humor, and love. Over the years, multiple back surgeries created physical challenges. But regardless of life's many obstacles, Melba has a way of bouncing back and moving forward. She is a wonderful reminder to us all that most of life's limitations live in our minds and that, with God, all things are possible because our true identity is found in Christ.

Dr. Melba Pattillo Beals's internal journey in life is as extraordinary as her external one. She inspires us all to be true to our own path, an assignment from God that we never fulfill alone.

Gerald Jampolsky, MD, founder of Attitudinal Healing and author of many books, including the international bestseller *Love Is Letting Go of Fear*

Diane Cirincione-Jampolsky, PhD, founder of Attitudinal Healing International

Acknowledgments

To my daughter, Dr. Kellie Beals, whose birth compelled me to grow up and to carve a decent life path, and to my sons, Matt and Evan Pattillo, who arrived in my life at my middle age and thereby refreshed my reasons for living and compelled me to expand rather than contract.

To Bret Baughman, who uses his machete sharpened with charm and grace to clear the way for me to find a home against the odds.

To George Buquich, an angel endowed with caregiving skills and rare early knowledge of the practice of being a son.

To Judie Fouchaux, my executive assistant, whose unending faith and positive energy keep me afloat when I have no other boat.

To Pauline and Richard France, whose prayers and consistent visits with Chinese food and table settings in hand kept me connected to the life I'd left due to my surgery and to which I wanted to return.

To Dr. Jann Garcia, who reached out to recruit me as her mom and instead ended up helping to parent me.

To Charles Gardiner, my daughter's partner, my son in love, who listens to me with patience and advises me with love and is never judgmental.

To all the members of the Little Rock Nine: Ernest Green, the late Jefferson Thomas, Gloria Ray Karlmark, Elizabeth Eckford, Thelma Mothershed Wair, Terrence Roberts, Minnijean Brown, and especially Carlotta Walls Lanier, who stood by me through my journey back to the past.

To my adoptive parents, George and Carol McCabe, and my adopted sisters and brother, Judy, Joan, Dori, and Rick, who taught me that equality is an inside job, the result of my willingness to claim it.

To Carol Normandy, a light along life's path for me and a benevolent angel to fuel my spiritual progress.

To the Pugh family, Herman, Esther, and their daughters, Vicki and DeeDee, who over the last twelve years have forged a family connection that brought me love and my only grandbabies to date.

Introduction

Grandma India always said that all human beings need something bigger and more powerful than themselves to believe in. It is best when we choose God, a specific and certain choice, whom we can trust to be our life companion. "If you have faith the size of a mustard seed, you know you are always safe. Even when you find yourself falling off the highest mountain, don't panic! Take stock to see what you can do to help yourself. If the answer is nothing, relax and enjoy the scenery, knowing that no matter how great the danger appears, you are safe in God's arms."

Growing up in the 1940s and '50s in Little Rock, Arkansas, I needed a powerful God and every drop of faith I could muster and sustain to hope that one day I would be free of the imprisoning bars of segregation. I longed to be free to go to the school of my choice, to sit in the front of the bus, to drink from the nearest water fountains not marked colored, to ride on the city park merry-go-round, and to walk the sidewalks downtown without being called ugly names. I longed to touch merchandise in stores without fearing someone would cut my hand off.

Grandma India said faith is the consistent trust that God is all powerful and always on your side if you need help. Throughout her life, she was a member of the Methodist church where I was baptized as a baby. She insisted that I remain respectful of all people and their methods of worshiping their God as I cling to my commitment to my God and Jesus Christ, the Son of God.

It would be my task to remain loyal to God, obeying His laws for living. "Taking time to study the Bible and obey your God will be crucial to your success," she said. "The warrior is the active part of you that helps you make things happen. God is always the energy of your warrior. He is as close as your skin, and you have only to call on Him for help."

By age three, I had memorized the Lord's Prayer and the 23rd Psalm, which she repeated to me every night as she tucked me into bed. There were several hymns and tons of Bible verses to memorize that specified the behavior God expected from me.

I regularly had personal talks with God because Grandmother promised I would be heard. When things went wrong, He would be with me, like when I found out my father might be leaving the family because he and Mom were not getting along. I decided that for me God would be an even bigger Dad, because I needed a dad to be with me always.

I went into the backyard and sat on the ground, leaning on the trunk of the big tree and holding on to my Raggedy Ann doll. I spoke to God, trying to hear what He would say to explain the word *divorce*. Who would protect us on those dark nights when the Klan rode in their white sheets, flashing their crosses and rifles and setting houses on fire? It would be okay, I heard God promise through my whimpers. It would be okay—He would keep me safe because He was God, my super strong Father, bigger and stronger than any Klan, more powerful than my human dad could be.

From the earliest age, I remember Grandma sticking individual pictures of my brother, mother, and me on our family refrigerator. She said they were there to demonstrate how much she loved us, how beautiful I was, and how handsome Brother was. Posted that way, she could look at us at all times of the day and appreciate how much we resembled God's heavenly angels, she said. Above all else, she declared, "God loves you. He has your pictures on His refrigerator just as I do."

One day when I was sad and crying over being called a nigger in the grocery store, Grandma said, "God loves you. He knows how beautiful you are. Don't crinkle that pretty little face. God doesn't know the word *nigger*, and He will be disappointed if you give in to it."

To this day, whenever I feel inconsolably sad, I remember that statement—God loves me so much that He has my picture on His refrigerator. I know I am beautiful because God thinks I am.

Without any doubt, my life experiences have taught me that Grandmother was correct. Indeed, I have learned that God is with me at all times. He has demonstrated over and over His love for me. If I am willing to believe in God, I can build a relationship with Him—one that includes faith, trust, and hope—that serves me when I most need it. I am never alone, never without the powerful resources He provides.

One

AN ANGEL WITH A BROOM

December days in Little Rock, Arkansas, are filled with a foggy ground chill that bites the bones, no matter how many coats and hats one wears. On December 1, 1941, my grandmother, India Peyton, was midway on a twelve-block walk to downtown in order to see a supervisor at Missouri Pacific Hospital. She was seeking permission for my mother to be given space in the maternity section because Mother Lois was about to give birth to me. Grandma worried that the bulge of my weight in her daughter's stomach far outweighed her capacity to birth me.

"White folks don't take kindly to the notion that one of us might be in their hospital. But because Daddy Howell was a worker there, there was some hope we could get your mother in. Your mother's belly was stretched bigger than God planned it to be," Grandma would later tell me.

Mother Lois was five feet four and weighed ninety-three pounds. Doctors estimated that I could weigh at least nine pounds. Grandmother had already been told that she would not be allowed to bring her daughter to the hospital, no matter the risk.

The previous morning, Grandmother India had been turned down again by the clerk. She requested to see a higher-ranking supervisor to plead for entry for Mom. Now a little more than halfway there, walking as fast as she could, she wondered whether she would ever get there. The fierce wind bit her legs and seared her cheeks. She felt as though it would knock her down. If she could have made the trip a little later, she could have ridden the bus. But at 5:30 in the morning, no buses were running. She could not risk being even a moment late for her 7:00 a.m. job as a maid at the hotel.

Protecting her face with her gloved hands, she tried hard to see what was in front of her. Grandmother decided that the only way she was going to complete her trip was to pray aloud the familiar Lord's Prayer. Upon arrival at the back door, the entry assigned to people of color, she wondered whether she had the strength to swing the heavy double doors with the strong wind blowing. Just then the door swung open for her, and Mr. Jeffers, the janitor, reached his hand out to her and pulled her inside to the warmth.

"Miss India, what on earth is a body doing out here in all this freezing weather?"

Taking off her glasses to clear the fog, she asked Mr. Jeffers to point her to Mr. Van Albor's office.

"Ohhh, Miss India, why you looking for him? He ain't gonna see nobody like us."

"I need to get doctoring for my baby. She's with child, and I want her to come here because the baby is really big. That baby weighs too much for her little body to carry."

"Oh Lord, you know they ain't gonna let that happen. The saying here is, if you let one in, they'll all think they're entitled to be here."

"I got no choice, Mr. Jeffers. I gotta save my baby's life."

She turned and walked toward the elevator, following his directions. On the third floor, there stood the huge wooden door that led to the hospital supervisor's office.

"I need Your help, dear Lord." She hesitated a moment to whisper her prayer before she knocked for permission to enter.

"Good morning, Aintee. I understand you want me to do the impossible."

"No, sir. I want you to please help me save my daughter's life. My son-in-law, Howell Pattillo, is a good man and is one of your workers here. He is a Hostler's helper on the Missouri Pacific Railroad."

"You're not asking for special treatment, are you? You know very well that Negras aren't coddled here."

Grandma winced because he used the familiar word *Negra*, which racist white folks called a compromise—a combination between nigger and Negro. She grasped control of herself as she squeezed her feeling tight in her throat. She could ill afford to offend him at this point.

"No, sir, of course not."

"The answer is no, Aintee. Why are you wasting my time?"

Grandma says her heart sank as she moved toward the door, and then she remembered what her pastor had instructed.

"Bishop Riley said I should ask because it is so important to save my daughter's life. She's a schoolteacher and a Christian. We and Bishop Riley would be grateful."

Grandmother's pastor had advised that the only possible way to get her daughter into the hospital was if Bishop Riley supported her. He was the only African American in our community who held sway over some members of the white community. Nobody seemed to know why, but everybody in our community knew it was just so.

"Aintee, now you know that there's no way I can give you a regular room. I'll allow her to stay here in a storage room. We have an empty room. So it's yours while it's empty. She needs to have that baby before a week passes. Do you hear me? A week."

"Oh, thank you, sir, thank you. I will report your kindness to the bishop."

"Hold on, Aintee. Don't get any ideas about inviting your relatives and friends to celebrate. Only you, the father, and the mother can come in that back door, and be quiet. Nobody needs to know you all are here."

"Yes, sir."

"And there will be no birth certificate saying that baby was born here. I don't want a parade of Negras marching here stinking up the place."

"Of course, sir."

Backing out of the office, curtseying with her hands in a praying position, Grandmother was very grateful.

On Saturday afternoon, December 6, Mother Lois began harsh, prolonged contractions and spurts of pain that overcame her. Papa dropped her and Grandma off just outside the hospital back door. Mother was in a small, windowless but clean room. She began what would become a long night and next day filled with drama and pain with Grandmother at her side. The room Mother occupied was down an isolated hallway. When Grandmother asked for pain medication, the nurse said, "Give you niggers an inch and you take a mile."

Early the next morning, Mother was wrenched with pain and covered with perspiration. Grandmother feared that nurses and doctors would ignore her. She telephoned Dr. Routen, a white doctor who had been our family doctor for several years. He came to the hospital and summoned another physician to give Mother medicine and take her to the delivery room.

Meanwhile, Dad discovered a radio down the hall and was busy going back and forth between the two rooms as he announced, "Pearl Harbor has been attacked."

December 7, 1941, was a traumatic day that looms in this country's history! Bombs were bursting in air as Pearl Harbor was shattered. Hearing announcements of this tragic event was secondary in Mother's life as she prepared to give birth to her first child.

Grandmother prayed and read Bible verses as Father meandered back and forth with news of Pearl Harbor. They anticipated a difficult birth. It lasted thirty hours. Mother Lois was petite—while Father was six feet four and two hundred pounds. As time grew near, Grandmother reported that there were signs of trouble. Dad was not called, as men were not allowed in the delivery room.

When the birth process grew ever more difficult, the doctor decided to use forceps, though admitting this practice could lead to infection. I weighed nine pounds, eight ounces.

After the birth was complete, Mom and I were taken to the storage room. On the way out, Grandma remembered seeing Mr. Jeffers cleaning the birth room.

By my first evening on earth, December 7, it was evident that my head was swelling, and I could not keep my tiny hands from scratching. Grandma said I cried all night long, but even though she pled with the nurse, no one would come to address my problem. By Monday, my temperature had soared to 103 degrees. My hot, swollen head was an open, bleeding wound, which alarmed Mother, Grandmother, and Father.

By Tuesday, December 9, my temperature was 105. The doctor announced that the infection was spreading, and I probably would not make it. He operated on my head and inserted irrigating tubes.

The next day, just outside Mother's door, Mr. Jeffers was sweeping the floor. When he heard Grandmother praying aloud as Mother cried softly, he stepped inside the door and expressed his concern. "I guess washing her head with that there Epsom salts did not work," he lamented.

"What Epsom salts?" Grandmother asked.

"The doctor told the nurse the baby's head needs rinsing every two hours or so with Epsom salts."

"No," Grandmother said, "the baby's been here with us, and the nurse has not come to rinse her head."

Racing down the hallway, Grandma got ahold of the nurse. "We do not coddle niggers here," the red-haired nurse shouted. "Understand I don't have time for you or your baby. You don't belong here!"

Grandmother grabbed her purse and left for the store to purchase Epsom salts. Only by the grace of God and an angel carrying a broom did I live. Three days later, we left the hospital.

As a child growing up, I always fretted about the bald strip that ran from the top of my misshapen head down to the right ear. I was so afraid that one of my friends would say something. Grandmother always quieted my fretting—explaining that it was proof of how special I was in God's eyes because He had saved my life against all odds. "God has been kind to give you beautiful hair like shiny black satin to cover your scar. No one will know," she said. "God has rescued you from death because He has special assignments for you. You will get word of the tasks you are to perform when He deems you ready for His work."

That special assignment came fifteen years later in September of 1957, when I was chosen as one of the Little Rock Nine—nine African American children selected by the National Association for the Advancement of Colored People (NAACP) to integrate Central High School in Little Rock, Arkansas, amid a firestorm of angry mobs determined to keep us out.

It was not until fifty years later that I learned the enormity of the blessing I was granted. A cranial specialist was to examine my head because I had felt some discomfort after I accidently caught my head when closing the car trunk. As the nurse entered the room to gather preliminary information, I greeted her. She examined my head and began talking loudly and slowly to me as though I was hard of hearing and mentally disabled.

"What day is it?" she shouted, leaning in close, staring at me.

"Tuesday," I said, curious about her behavior.

"Who is president?" she screeched.

"President Clinton, William Jefferson Clinton," I repeated.

At first, I cooperated with her line of questions, but then I screamed, "Lady, I am a professor with a doctoral degree. How can I help you?"

That is when, with an astonished expression, she explained to me that with my misshapen head and the nature of the injury, I could have suffered cerebral palsy or another severe brain injury. The doctor said I was a walking miracle. I whispered, "Thank You, God," all the way back to the car.

What I know for sure is that we have a God who guides and protects us. God is always available when we call for help and even when we are unable or unwilling to call. He intervenes to rescue us, even when we don't know we need help.

Two

WALKING THROUGH THE VALLEY

Growing up in segregated Little Rock, Arkansas, in the 1950s was a deep life and faith struggle for a person of color. The first emotion I was aware of was fear. Fear of what would happen if we disobeyed the rules connected to large signs placed everywhere that read Whites Only, Black Folks Not Welcome. By the age of three, I noticed that white people were in charge, because they were the ones who kept telling the grown-ups in my family what to do. Every time we encountered them, my mom, dad, and grandma behaved as though they were really nervous and frightened they might do something wrong. Their fears were contagious because I mimicked that fear as well. Whenever we were near white people or even any of our relatives who were white-skinned and blue-eyed, I was terrified. So much so that when my blue-eyed cousins came to babysit us, I hid in the closet or under the bed.

At age five, I joined in with the adults and complained about white folks being in charge because I resented not being able to ride the merry-go-round, sit in movies, or swim in the city pools. "Why can't God make them share?" I asked over and over again. "We could each be in charge half a year. Put them in charge from January to June and give my folks charge from July to December."

"In God's time," Grandma replied. "Be patient. God loves you. Trust and He will provide."

Following the 1954 decision by the US Supreme Court that separate is *not* equal and that all public schools must be open to all children, the NAACP demanded that Arkansas's formerly all-white schools comply. Little Rock school officials announced that they would comply with the court order by choosing African American children to enter the all-white Central High. I was selected as one of the first nine teenagers to enter that prestigious white school, which had a student body of more than nineteen hundred.

Suddenly, in early September 1957, the city that had been my home for most of my life turned into an armed camp with hundreds of folks gathering in front of Central High each morning with the intent of keeping the nine of us out. After a few days, the press was describing this gathering as a mob—a rampaging, out-of-control mob. News reporters from around the world were arriving in my hometown, focusing on what was becoming a volatile battle between our US government and the state of Arkansas, and I was in the middle of it.

At the tender age of fifteen, my struggles to share equal opportunities would become a primer for my understanding of faith. Being able to sustain myself through a school year fraught with drama, violence, and fear was a critical tool in faith building. Integrating Central High School would become the foundation for a lifetime of sustaining faith and trust. That experience enabled me to embark upon a journey of life's challenges with the confidence that Jesus would always be at my side.

A shouting, angry, rock-throwing mob continued to block the entryway to Central High School during early September and the beginning of classes. As always, the Ku Klux Klan rode at night, only now more frequently in our neighborhood, violently threatening random people from our community because we wanted to attend their school. Unfortunately, news reports listed our addresses and phone numbers. I began receiving threatening and vulgar phone calls day and night. Shots rang out, and bullets pierced our window, shattering Grandmother's antique flower vase, which stood on top of our television.

Due to the escalating violence, I was no longer a cheerful teenager enjoying the Saturday night Hit Parade of music on television or waiting to hear Johnny Mathis sing on the radio or gathering at our community center to chat, play games, or take dance lessons. Instead, I was forbidden to leave the house without appropriate adult escorts. The only time I saw other teenagers was at church. My social life was crammed with press conferences and official meetings with the eight others who shared my predicament. These integration strategy meetings and lectures from Arkansas school officials were to tell us what we could and could not do—for example, "Don't antagonize white students by drinking from Central High water fountains; bring a canteen of water in your lunch bucket. Never hit back!"

As grateful as I was for the kind, respectful, and considerate Quakers who traveled from far away to help us, I became frightened of their nonviolent lectures and demonstrations of how to turn the other cheek or stop, drop, and roll. It would be much later that gratitude to them would overwhelm me because there was no doubt that their teaching helped to save our lives. Added to the changes usurping my social schedule were the parental meetings instructing us on how to duck, hide, or escape should the Klan choose to visit our home unannounced, brandishing their rifles and burning crosses.

Amid a growing whirlwind of unfamiliar activities, places, people, and instructions, I felt distressed. I could clearly hear Grandma's advice round the clock as though filed on cards in my head: "If you are going to have genuine faith, you must be certain of the purpose for your work and what you want to accomplish—what is your goal? Intent and purpose dictate your warrior action. Is your activity the same as God's wishes? You must know the answer to that question without any doubt."

Hour after hour, I sat pondering those questions as my life began to have little resemblance to that which I was accustomed. Even when my younger brother, Conrad, begged me to play a game with him or Mother Lois admonished me for not reading enough literature, I couldn't refocus.

Following the Supreme Court ruling in 1954, and in the ninth grade at the time, I had raised my hand to volunteer to go to Central High because it was in my neighborhood. I was curious as to why I was never allowed to go there before. I attended a moderate, one-story high school, at which white students dumped their used books and broken-key typewriters at the end of the school semester.

Each Sunday after church, Mother took us on a ride past the magnificent Central High with its seven stories, manicured lawns, distinct topiary, and granite water fountains. I had always been told that this giant, eight-square-block institution was filled with opportunities for a better education. The Little Rock School District automatically reserved for them fancier supplies, such as new equipment, advanced typewriters, an enormous band pit, and real apartments for practicing home economics. Our school received what they discarded—broken junk.

The African American folk who cooked in Central High talked about the miracles offered in that gigantic compound with all its vast space, modern equipment, outdoor sports fields, and giant auditorium. I thought going there would bring blessings because it would provide me with an opportunity to get a scholarship to one of the top universities in the country. Attending Central High would be my ticket to escape from Little Rock forever.

Questions hung in the air for us. When should we nine enter Central, how should we go, and with whom? All schools were about to be officially in session. Meetings revolved around the school board coordinating plans with the NAACP, which had to coordinate plans with our parents. With rising tensions fed by segregationists who opposed integration, it was clear we would need some kind of protection to get past the mob. All the threats from segregationists across the South and the confusion festering in my own community mixed into a keg of dynamite waiting to be ignited by fear and anger. I began asking myself if I had enough faith in my God to keep me safe from the bullies who seemed so powerful and determined to keep us out. My time alone in my room was spent being afraid and praying for relief.

Although we had spent the latter part of August 1957 meeting and planning, the ultimate phone call came from the national NAACP representative late on September 1. She instructed Mother and me to meet the others the next day on the corner of 14th Street and Park and to walk toward the center of the school on 15th. The front of Central was two blocks long. I had no words to describe what I was feeling or thinking as I prepared for my first day of seeing what was inside this huge castle forbidden to me for so long and that I had daydreamed about.

To add to the complexity of the drama, the night before we were to go to school, Governor Faubus suddenly posted Arkansas National Guard troops encircling the school. Newspapers, radio, and television were filled with talk of us and our going to Central High. No one seemed certain about what the soldiers were there to do—tame the mob, protect us and provide safe passage through the mob, or as one of the reporters predicted, merely provide pretty television pictures? Somehow the NAACP assumed the soldiers were there to keep peace. After all, Faubus bragged that he was the governor of *all* the people.

It was a warm, muggy day as Mom and I headed for the school expecting some news reporters and confusion. Instead, we wandered, unaware, into a hornet's nest. We noted the huge crowd gathered on the street directly across from Central High School, their attention focused on the front of the school. We had asked ourselves why at 7:30 in the morning the streets that led us there were so clogged with traffic and throngs of people—walking and driving. We were panicked because there was no place for us to park. We were late to meet the others, and once on foot, we did not see anyone we knew. We had thought there would be NAACP officials and school board members there as guides, but instead there was a sea of white faces—red, angry white faces. It was like attending a parade or a huge football game uninvited.

In hindsight, had we been more conscious of the situation, we would have known for certain we were in grave danger. Not realizing our predicament, however, we struggled to make our way into the center of the crowd, preoccupied with finding a familiar face. We attempted to follow the instructions about entering Central High, which we now realized were vague.

Making our way through a sardine-like packed crowd, we found ourselves deep in the middle of a multilayer of humanity, all white, focused on whatever was across the street. As we drew near, I cupped my hands around my eyes to see what they were focused on. Amid loud calls for "hang that nigger" was Elizabeth Eckford, one of us. The huge crowd was directing their hostility toward her as she stood alone. She was across the street from us directly in front of Central High, facing the long line of soldiers and surrounded by a barking cluster of white people who were screeching at her back.

Barely five feet tall, my friend Elizabeth cradled her books in her arms as she desperately searched for the right place to enter. Uniformed soldiers towered over her and closed ranks each time she tried to enter the concrete walkway to the front door. Walking first to one and then another soldier, she seemed determined to walk between them, but they were just as determined to keep her away from the front door. She stood erect and proud as she turned away, concluding that she would not get through.

Elizabeth walked along the line of soldiers. They did nothing to protect her from the shouting people on her heels who were spitting on her, yelling in her ear, calling her names. As a crowd of hecklers attempted to close in, the soldiers stared straight ahead. The human vultures around her seemed unwilling to give up. At that instant when the soldiers closed rank, she stood still, not knowing what to do. The people near us stomped and shouted louder as though gratified by her predicament. "Get her, get the nigger and hang her black behind." Others applauded and goaded those who were preparing to go after Elizabeth.

Fear swallowed me within a weird cloud because I needed to go to where she stood. But where should we go? Elizabeth slowly wedged her way past those surrounding her and headed for the corner where there was a bus stop. She did not react to what was happening around her but instead appeared to be staring straight ahead as she walked rather than ran at a confident pace. She reached the bus bench at the corner and sat down. Thank God, a white female, Mrs. Grace Lorch, and Benjamin Fine from the *New York Times* sat on either side of her, protecting her from would-be attackers.

Is that what I would have to do? What would happen to us? Mother and I wanted to cross the street and help her, but the shock of what we were seeing momentarily froze us in our tracks. Suddenly, the men around us shouted, "We got us a nigger right here." That's when Mother and I realized we were in great danger as well. We began to edge our way backward.

All at once, a white man glowered at me and grabbed my sleeve. I snatched my arm away and lunged toward the rear of the crowd. The men gathering around us carried ropes

34

and weapons. The man who had grabbed at me began telling those around him that Mom and I were nearby. Mother and I tugged at each other and sped up our pace. We bumped into people and pushed through harder. "We got us a nigger right here," someone shouted again.

"They're getting away," another man yelled. "The niggers are getting away." Reaching the sidewalk path, I was bumping hard into people with my determination to escape. I began to realize for certain they wanted to kill me. The path was not paved but was rather partially dirt with chunks of concrete and tree stumps.

The men who chased us began saying aloud their plans for us—how they wanted to have their way with us and then hang us. I had never felt that kind of fear before. It nested in the lining of my stomach, moving upward into my throat. I had an urge to call out for help, but who would save me? There was no one there who cared about me. Mom and I were alone. Police had stood by watching Elizabeth in peril and done nothing. I knew for certain they would not help me.

"Take these keys," Mom said in a commanding voice. "You get to the car and leave me here."

"No, Mom, no!" For the first time in my life, I felt the burn of her hand as she slapped me on my cheek. I didn't know how to disobey her, but I wasn't going to leave her there. I was a few feet in front of her. Circling back to grab her arm, I wouldn't let her go. She must have been getting tired because she was slowing down. I was pulling her and running as fast as I could.

Just then a man grabbed the back of her suit jacket to pull her back. Holding on to her briefcase with one hand, she wiggled out of the jacket. I knew we were going to die, right there together, if I didn't do something. But what? We were only steps ahead of the men—just steps. I recalled Grandmother's words: "God is as close to you as your skin. You have but to ask, and He will reach out to help you." I began to repeat aloud the words of the Lord's Prayer and the 23rd Psalm.

Down on the unpaved path in front of us were dead tree branches that Mother and I went around. The men directly behind us did not see them, and they tumbled over each other. "Please, God, please," I whispered. Their fall gave us the few seconds we needed to get to the car. I made it into the driver's side and turned the key. Although I had driven very little, I put the car into reverse and backed out of that space faster than I had ever driven forward.

As we backed away, a cluster of men were banging on our front windshield. I continued repeating the Lord's Prayer and the 23rd Psalm under my breath as I drove backward through a hail of rocks and shouts. Speeding up, I circled around to go forward and went five blocks or so before realizing that everything was all right now and that, above all else, Grandma was right. God had made a miracle of branches on the ground, and we were safe—safe from the mob determined to kill us—for now.

That night after we settled down safe at home, with doors and windows locked and shades drawn, I realized I could not get on my knees and merely say the Lord's Prayer as usual. I had to say something special to God because He had done something special at my request. He had come to my aid and helped me when I called. There was no doubt in my mind that God had heard me. It was the first time God became real in my life. He was no longer words on the page of a hymnal and in the Bible. He was real, alive, and demonstrating His love for me.

For the first time in my life, I felt I had direct connection to a God who was mine to keep. I began my prayers by talking to God as though He was my friend. "I have never been that frightened. I didn't know what I needed to do to stay alive. Do You really want me to go to Central High? If so, please come with me, please keep me safe. Was Your help today a sign that I should move ahead or that I should withdraw and go back to my old high school? I love You, God. Thank You, thank You, and thank You for hearing me."

I felt a presence as though there was a warm blanket of love around me and someone in the room whom I could not see. After wading through many thoughts, I asked God not to go away because I would certainly need Him again. I was going to get inside Central High and try to complete the year there. From that moment forward, I would have faith that my God would be my real companion. I promised Him I would listen for His assignments for me. My faith was now bigger than a mustard seed, and I had hope I could complete His assignment.

As my grandma had promised, God is as close to us as our skin, and it's up to us to call on Him if we need help.

Three

ANGELS IN COMBAT BOOTS

After we were driven away from Central High School on the first day by an angry mob determined that we not integrate the school, the big question was whether I would return. Would my parents decide yes, and would the courts rule?

Our house was filled with what we called God's revival discussions about whether I was meant to go ahead with my attendance at Central High. The danger everyone had imagined had become a reality. Grandma was calling her prayer circle, asking for prayer sessions twice a day so we could keep on the Lord's path and stay safe. A big part of the discussion was whether this was God's intent for me, considering the growing danger for both me and the family as each day went by.

Father said he wanted me taken out of school and flown to be with his relatives on the East Coast. Mother said this was a possibility we needed to ponder because we had no practice in dealing with what was becoming a constant world of fear. Ultimately, Grandmother concluded that if I had been chosen out of all those hundreds of students who applied and if I had a burning desire to change the direction of life for our people in Little Rock, I should take this God-given opportunity. That is when she turned to Mom and said, "Are we a faith family or have we given up trusting God for His protection? Isn't that the bottom line? When you go, Melba, God will be with you." The NAACP called a meeting and ordered us not to return to Central High until they called us. We would spend the days that followed out of school while all our friends started their semester.

Because the governor had called back the National Guard and was now using state troopers to keep us from returning to Central High, the NAACP went to court seeking an injunction to prohibit the governor from blocking our entry. I was frightened that Friday as I sat in the hot courtroom, crowded with lawyers and hordes of news reporters, that the judge might not grant such an order. After much bickering and objection by lawyers for the governor, the judge ruled we could return to the school.

The next time we attempted to enter Central High was Monday, September 23, 1957. We were given rides by our parents, who dropped us off at the side entrance in accordance with instructions from the NAACP. Members of the Little Rock police force were to escort us into the 14th Street side door. As we pulled up to the curb, I caught a fleeting glimpse of the screeching crowd, sounding like the roar of a huge football game, gathered at the corner half a block away. They were clustered behind wooden sawhorses with policemen standing guard. Their presence was different this time. Before, there were fewer policemen and nothing to hold the mob back. This crowd was more frightening, however, because their number had grown even larger.

As I was getting out of the passenger side of the car, a uniformed officer beckoned to me. Two of them walked our group up the stairs to the side door, where we were greeted by a stocky woman with a grim expression and dark brown hair. Once we were inside, she directed us to climb up a few more stairs to the two-block-long, curved hallway filled with hostile, red-faced students growling their unwelcome. With its wide expanse and tall ceilings, the hallway was dimly lit. Nevertheless, I could see our guide's facial expression. She did not have a smile and cheerful good morning for us but, instead, mumbled crunchy words that came from the mouth of a scowling face.

We made our way to what I assumed was the center of the hallway—about three-fourths of a block into the stately marble-floored passageway—where the central office was located. At that point, I was counting on the fact that although we nine African American students were surrounded by mostly very angry white people, some of them must be educated like my mom and some must worship a God of some description and have compassion for us. I was wrong. Not one of them showed any sign of welcome. Later I would decide that perhaps the peer pressure of that large student body was great, and no one could afford to show us any kindness.

After we received our class assignments, I asked Principal Matthews, "Excuse me, sir, why aren't any of us assigned to classes together?"

"You kids want integration, we'll give you integration. You will go nine separate ways." Even Thelma Mothershed, the one among us who was admittedly a bit disabled by her heart condition, was sent off in a different direction. Almost immediately, their expressions, the attitudes of the school officials, and the spoken words of the principal let me know they were angry enough to do something drastic to get us kicked out. We could definitely not count on them for protection or even a civil hello.

With a Pillsbury Doughboy sarcastic smile, the principal ushered us out the office doors. Stunned by the prospect of our group being split nine different ways, I felt tears bubbling in my throat. I dared not display them in my eyes, but I had to admit I was frightened in a way I had never felt before.

Recalling the promise that God is my companion, I squared my shoulders, stood up straight, and reached somewhere deep down inside for courage. Determined not to show emotion, I moved ahead. I realized that no matter who I thought was assigned to protect me, I could depend on only myself and my God. If I was to make it through the next minute, the next hour, and the next day, I needed to upgrade my faith and trust.

Each of us was assigned a guide to negotiate the gigantic building. I was totally silent as my guide urged me to ascend the stairs. I had no choice but to turn to the Lord's Prayer for strength to climb to the third floor where my homeroom was located. Over and over again, I whispered the prayer under my breath. By the time I entered classroom 313, I had repeated it thirteen and a half times. I would practice that ritual throughout the school year in order to keep myself inspired to move with dispatch.

Walking among so many people, the majority of whom were mistreating me, was a new experience for me. Sometimes I felt as though I were a dartboard and everyone was shooting darts at me, some aiming at my heart, some at my head, and all really hurting me. At other times, I felt as though I were the food one drops into a fish tank that all the fish suddenly dive toward. All the voices in my head were shouting, *Run, run, get out of here; you will die if you stay here.*

Still, I knew for certain I could not run. I had to calm myself down and all the while give the impression I was strong and able to cope. I had no place to go except inside myself for comfort and hope. Part of me was listening to the incredible shouting in the background, the voices of the mob outside. What was going to happen with them? Thank God the police were holding them back with the sawhorses.

Gathering strength, I continued making my way through the jungle of angry humankind. At 11:30 that day, school officials summoned us to return to the first-floor office. As I descended the stairs, I was filled with questions: What now? What did they want of us? Upon reaching the office, I followed the same school administrator who, though still not introducing herself, had escorted us earlier that morning through an inner office and past very official-looking white men. I was alarmed by the anxious expressions on their faces. I was led to an adjoining anteroom—a smaller office where some of the other eight had gathered. Two of the girls were crying. I stood near the door, which was ajar enough so that although I could not see who was speaking, I could hear much of the men's conversations. I heard their frantic tone of voice, heard them say the mob was out of control and that they would have to call for help. "What are we gonna do about the nigger children?" asked one.

"The crowd is moving fast. They've broken the barricades. These kids are trapped in here."

"Good Lord, you're right," another voice said. "We may have to let the mob have one of these kids so we can distract them long enough to get the others out."

Shortly after, a tall man who identified himself as an assistant police chief entered the room and did not mince words. "You Negro students must leave Central High School right now. Members of the mob are moving toward the school."

With so many police around, shouldn't they be able to protect us? Imagining what must be going on outside made me even more frightened. The fear rising in a frothing ball in my stomach was beyond anything I had ever experienced before. There were no words to describe the feelings that engulfed me and made my knees shake. I knew for certain that no one was coming to rescue me. If the police couldn't save me, who was capable of getting me past that mob? I couldn't think of any human being who could. Only God could help me. "May we call our parents?" I asked.

"No, no, we don't have time."

Call God, the voice in my head said over and over again.

Two white policemen hurriedly ushered us out of the office, through a heavy wooden door, and down a winding staircase that led through a dark passage to the basement. I hesitated, closing my eyes, hoping for divine assurance.

My inner warrior was rising inside me—something had to be done. Were they leading us into a trap in which we would surely die in order for them to gain favor with the mob? What choice did I have? I began repeating the Lord's Prayer, whispering it under my breath as I scurried as fast as I could to keep up. I would have to believe what Grandma promised me, that God is as close to me as my skin and always stronger than any enemy.

As we descended the stairs to a dimly lit basement, I couldn't help asking myself whether I should try to run toward the sliver of light piercing through huge doors hung on gigantic chains. But how would I get them open? There were policemen with us who were bigger and stronger and carrying guns. Pausing for a moment, I pleaded with God, "Again, I ask You to please help all of us out of this—please, please. I don't know what You can do, but help . . . help."

I realized that beyond that door were some of the same yowling voices I heard from the mob across the street—the same calls for "get the niggers."

We were shepherded into waiting police cars and, once inside, were told to put our heads down on our laps as we climbed up the concrete driveway out of the basement. Members of the mob had taken up a station there at the side of the school, armed with weapons and more intention to hurt us. Hearing the shouts and rocks and other objects banging on the car frightened me beyond words. "Please, God, help me," I whispered.

I could feel my heart pounding in my chest; every other sound was drowned out by shouting people around me. I felt the car moving and looked up to see the hands and faces of people against our windshield as members of the mob grabbed for the car, hoping to stop it and have their way with us.

For a time, the car only crept along, and I realized we were somewhat trapped because the police could not afford to injure anyone in that crowd. I thought the awful crowd had us at its mercy as we slowly crawled along. I held my ears and prayed that the locks kept the doors shut. I don't know how many times I repeated the Lord's Prayer before I could hear the engine of the car over the shouts of the crowd. With the escort of the kind police, God had helped us escape our predators. God had answered my prayer once more.

When I arrived home, I hopped out of the car to greet Grandmother and neighbors who were in a panic. "We heard that the mob got hold of you," shouted Mrs. Brooks, the neighbor from across the street. "Praise God you made it."

That Monday evening, even bigger crowds rampaged, causing incredible havoc. Tuesday, the violent rampages were bigger and louder. Following all that drama, our city became an armed camp, and I could not go anywhere unaccompanied by an adult. For that day, the mob had won. They were the reason we were forced to leave. Most of all, they frightened me into questioning whether I would ever return to high school again without drastic changes. Nevertheless, I tried to hold on to my faith and to the hope that the problem could be worked out. Someday I would get into Central High School and actually become a welcomed student there, if it was God's will.

The call came that evening from the NAACP—suspend, do not return to Central High until the call comes to do so. How could we possibly go back inside the school if the mob continued to gather in front and threaten us? I was, for the first time in my life, truly afraid of dying at their hands—all those people, all that hate, were like a huge army to face. I did not see how God could be bigger than the mob. And yet Grandma had always said that having faith was belief in a positive outcome, whether I could clearly see the outcome or not.

I couldn't imagine how God could keep us safe. What could He do to make the crowd go away? How could He convince them that it was all right for us to attend Central High, that we would not bother them or ruin what they had for generations considered their private sanctuary? The Monday we entered school and remained inside until almost noon became known across the world as Mob Monday. That evening as I was pondering what to do next, as were all the adults in meetings elsewhere, an announcement came over the airwaves that President Eisenhower would address the nation: his topic, the Little Rock school crisis.

To everyone's astonishment, the president announced he would be dispatching the famed 101st Airborne Division of the US Army—the Screaming Eagles, the heroes of the Korean War—to guard us and keep the peace.

Answers to our prayers may not always appear in the form we imagine. Sometimes God sends angels in combat boots to protect us.

Four

THROUGH TRIALS
AND TRIBULATIONS

On Wednesday morning, September 25, escorted by armed 101st Division soldiers, with helicopters overhead and troopers galloping back and forth across the two blocks in front of Central High School, we nine black children climbed up to the front door and walked inside. We got past a mob with God and the soldiers as our shields. We completed the day inside the school, not without incident but certainly with determination. That day, I learned it was going to require an enormous amount of faith for us to survive. We would have to turn the other cheek to verbal and physical abuse. That day, I confronted for the first time the reality of what I was facing, and I questioned whether I had what it took to live through the integration process over the long haul.

That evening, I thanked God for what was a miracle day. The presence of the soldiers did not totally convince the bullies to back off, but it was evident they were compelled to abandon some of their vicious activity. With personal bodyguards at our side—two soldiers each—and hallways full of uniformed men, I hoped that students would have a period to get to know us and to see that we meant them no harm but were there solely to get a good education just as they were.

However, after two days, we nine came to realize that the presence of the soldiers was not viewed by the segregationists' camp as a call for peace but instead as a declaration of war. The white Mothers' Citizen Council, an arm of the Klan, set up a training school to teach Central High students how to torture us.

Only a few of the vast number of soldiers of the 101st whom we saw were men of color, and none of these men guarded us. Our guards were always white. There was also the incredible realization that we were being guarded by some young men the exact same age as the Central High seniors. According to the local press, at night when they weren't guarding us, some of them were dating the female Central High students.

Although this was worrisome information, Grandmother said I must continue to have faith. "The very presence of the soldiers is a real miracle. Rarely has any president in United States history sent soldiers to intervene in city or state business." She called them "angels in combat boots" and promised that they were in this country's uniform and therefore would abide by the rules and regulations that governed their being chosen as a part of the Special Forces.

Indeed, those soldiers did live up to their commitment and their reputation as a disciplined unit. Despite trials and tribulations, acid in my eyes that would compromise my sight to this day, raw egg on my head, flag points piercing my back, and an array of torturous acts perpetrated on all nine of us, eight of us made it through, by the grace of God. To endure their behavior, I was able to build a wealth of faith and hone my practice of trusting God. The daily activities that frightened and discouraged me also compelled me to trust God. As it turned out, that Central High process would be my primer on faith and trust, providing the foundation for the rest of my life.

With gratitude for having gotten inside Central, I realized from the beginning that nothing about attendance resembled my former life in our old high school. My life changed so completely that I hardly recognized it. At first, there was excitement, astonishment, and delight at all the media attention I was getting. My pictures were on national television; President Eisenhower had written me a letter promising that if I returned to Central High, I would be protected by the troops. But it wasn't quite that easy. The segregationists did not accept the authority of the soldiers. Attending school became a daily dose of agony that I strained to endure.

Then the realization hit me. The pain and torture were continuous during time spent inside the school. That was minimally seven hours each day. Add to that travel time, exit and entry times, and time spent in meetings, and I concluded my entire life was now wrapped around the word *integration*. I wasn't at all certain I had understood how huge the task would be.

"Why me, God?" I asked over and over. "Why me?" I woke up with that question on my mind each day and heard it repeated in my head whenever there was a space between

51

the stressful activities filling my day. It was puzzling to me that the white students were not one iota more accepting as time passed, and I prayed harder and harder. Why had there been no effort on their part to quell their bullying behavior? Why did they not see that we were humans with innocent tasks to perform?

The students remained violent and unwelcoming, with few exceptions. Of the nineteen-hundred-plus students, some seemed willing to step forward and speak up against the primitive behavior. Those who did also suffered at the hands of their fellow students. Where were the adults, Christians, ministers from their community meant to civilize them? Their uncivilized behavior was true one week later and one month later. I felt their violent wrath grow bigger and bigger, energized by even more hatred each and every day.

After a few days, I became obsessed with trying to anticipate what awful atrocity they would launch next, especially in bathrooms, during gym class, and in the classroom because no soldiers were present there. I became obsessed with questions: How would I be injured? Where would I be injured? When would I be injured? Where on my body would I feel pain? When would I die? I felt my thoughts spinning out of control, but I had no one to speak to about my feelings.

One of the major weights I felt on my mind was the expectations adults had of us—not just our parents but NAACP attorneys who had dedicated their lives to working on ending segregation, people who read newspapers, lots of people we had never met. How could I disappoint them? I was becoming sadder each day. I was more uncertain of why I was so determined to attend that school and if all that I hoped to accomplish was equal to enduring so much suffering.

Was my graduation from that top-rated high school and the opportunity it offered to fulfill my dream of getting into a highly rated California university worth all the punishment I was suffering? I'd heard from friends how much different things were in California, how things were freer and happier there. To say that I was often very unhappy was an understatement. I held my breath, waiting for the weekends, hoping I could have fun with other African American friends who were leading normal lives. I was shocked to find that, after a few weeks, most African American students from our old high school began to shut us out.

Their parents were concerned about their safety. They too were being threatened because we were integrating Central, so they questioned integration itself. We had little time for normal teenaged socializing. What with homework, talking with the press, and meeting the NAACP obligations, I found myself exhausted from activity I did not find entertaining. I was not certain that I could generate the strength it took to make it through another hour, another day, or another week, let alone through two semesters.

I prayed so hard, spending the weekend on my knees, in church, or with my face in the Bible. Grandma's words began to stand out in my mind: "Wouldn't the best revenge be to remain there the entire year, to compel them to open their schools to people of color in the future, to graduate from Central? Many more of our people would get that because you first opened that door. How would striking back, escaping, or being thrown out make you feel? It hurts now, but I promise you there will be a time in the future when you will have joy when you think of this time. You will be grateful for all you have endured. You will be a strong warrior and so much readier to deal with life as it comes after this event."

Looking up into Grandmother's eyes, I couldn't imagine I could have joy when speaking of Central High School and my days there. None of what she promised made sense, but I trusted in the tone of her voice and the light in her eyes. In my heart, I knew she knew the truth, and I had to trust her. She gave me hope—hope that there could be a time when I felt normal again. There would be a time when the fear that was drowning me would turn into my ability to overcome fear in all my life. It was her tight, warm hug that gave me enough magic elixir to move forward.

Finally, she instructed me, "Faith is patience and trust that God knows exactly what He is doing, and since He cares about you and your future, you will eventually know that this was the right thing to do. It is God's plan that prevails—not yours." Grandmother pointed out passages in the Bible that said to be patient and wait on the Lord.

I couldn't help speculating how the change in all the bullies and haters might come about. Would it simply happen over a weekend, or would it be the result of something major, like the president making a decree of some type? How could the white students of Central High—all nineteen hundred of them—be made to see us as equals? We didn't want special treatment; we didn't want them to be our best friends. They could simply stop calling us names and hitting and kicking us, simply leave us alone. The problem was, I was waiting for them to change. Then one day it dawned on me. If segregationists had gone on for ages without changing their hideous behavior, then why would they now, why for me?

Meanwhile, with each passing day I began to settle down a bit, which reduced the fear somewhat. We regularly held meetings with dignitaries of the NAACP or ministers from all over the United States. On one particular evening, it was Dr. Martin Luther King Jr. who joined us in the home of local NAACP president, Mrs. Daisy Bates. I had read about his work in freeing our people and teaching equality. I was very honored that this noted civil rights leader would come to see us. He was so stately, so calm, so centered in a generous, loving attitude. He was to me undoubtedly a fearless, chosen angel.

At this point we were three weeks into the semester at Central High, and I was exhausted, depressed, and disappointed. I was still in shock at the price integrating that high school was exacting from me. I was somehow convinced someone would change things in an instant, so I couldn't stop myself from spilling my feelings about how much I was suffering to Dr. King. His quick answer was loud and clear as his huge eyes held mine with a commanding stare.

"Melba, don't be selfish. You're not doing this for yourself. You are doing this for generations yet unborn." His voice was kind, his face empathetic. Still, as he spoke, I first felt embarrassed, ashamed, and guilty for expressing my feelings. But he went on to explain to me the nature of a God-assigned task and surrender and patience. I had been waiting for white students to change, extend kindness, and welcome me, when maybe it was my task to change.

His statement jolted my thought process. I had to think long and hard about other students of color—other African American and Asian and Hispanic students—who would benefit from attending Central High with its academic advantages and equipment, and new, clean books, and many opportunities. The questions hanging in the air were, how much had I thought about them and how much did I really care about their needs? Was I being selfish to focus only on my needs? Dr. King's statement was life-changing.

As my days became tedious exercises in survival, my military bodyguard compared them to army warrior combat. He suggested I stop obsessing about what was going to happen and focus on surviving now. At first, it was very hard to do, but my 101st bodyguard helped me adapt my fears into survival techniques. Many times he reminded me that at no time during the day did I have time to ponder or to cry—I had to keep alert to my surroundings and keep moving. He told me I would have to develop specific techniques for coping with the day-to-day attacks.

A hymn Grandmother sang endlessly, "I Am on the Battlefield for My Lord," began to provide fresh hope for my mind. I had heard her sing it over and over as long as I had been on this earth. She sang with a smile, and now I listened closely each time. Surviving was the best revenge. If I could learn to console myself, to elevate my thoughts to think of the bullies' antics as a game—then I could win, and the winner takes all. Integration would begin officially after this year if I won, or the school would go back to segregation if they won. Integration couldn't be just for me; it had to be for a lot of other people who suffered. Segregation took away opportunities for a decent education and good jobs, but most of all it took away self-confidence. I began seriously thinking about all the ways attending that school could improve the lives of many students now and maybe my younger cousins in the future.

I could feel something growing inside me that I had never felt before. I vowed I would make it until Christmas vacation when I would have two weeks off and time to think. During a prayer chat with God, I shared my promise with Him and myself aloud.

By the beginning of November, we nine no longer had 101st soldier bodyguards accompanying us throughout the day. Instead, they were left to observe us from afar. If a big dispute erupted, they would step in. By the end of November, the 101st soldiers had gone back to their base in Kentucky. This was a time when I learned I could soothe my fears and keep them from boiling over by simply repeating the 23rd Psalm with every breath. With the bodyguards gone, I was overcome once again with trying to figure out what the students were going to do to me. Instead, I needed to be focusing on my immediate needs.

While preparing Thanksgiving dinner, Grandmother introduced me to two more crucial elements, two more of what she called the lynchpins in trust—*gratitude* and *forgiveness*. She explained that no matter what happens, I need to express my gratitude, knowing that whatever takes place has some piece in the ultimate puzzle that is the plan for my life.

At first, I was very annoyed at the suggestion that I should be grateful for the hurtful things that occurred in my day, all day. What was there to be grateful for? Still, she insisted I find things to be grateful for each day. Perhaps the hardest part of Grandmother's instruction was to forgive those who mistreated me at school.

It would take years for me to understand that the Central High experience put a core of steel in my spine—giving me strength, hope, and understanding far beyond my years. It was indeed an experience that would prepare me to go through the trials and tribulations of life with a unique perspective.

Forgiveness, she explained, is necessary to prevent one from living a life of chewing lemons. A failure to forgive leads to bitterness. While you are still holding on to a grudge, chewing a sour lemon and wincing from the bitter taste, the person you pinpoint for your wrath, believing your differences have been resolved, may well have forgotten all about it. Forgiveness opens your heart—and clears space to enjoy blessings.

Above all else, she instructed, "Keep your purposes in mind. You are there to help others as well as yourself!"

———

Our purpose must be clear. Purpose means doing God's work. It can never be activity for selfish reasons alone. There must be some share of gifting and contributing.

Five

FINDING MY INNER WARRIOR

I was determined was to remain a Central High student to complete my task of integration. I focused on putting as much of my energy as possible into coping mechanisms for surviving the abuse of each day. Faith, trust, and hope became the reasons I could get up, get dressed, and return to school each day for a day of misery. I began to have faith that I was willing to take the awful punishment in order to do God's work because it was what He wanted. I started to trust that God would certainly support me in an assignment He approved of, and therefore the situation would improve sooner rather than later.

I felt the emergence of my warrior, the inner voice that energized me and affirmed that I was doing God's work amid the harsh name-calling and frequent blows. The most frightening time was when I needed to use the girls' room, for the guards could only stand a few feet outside the door. Sitting in the cubicle, I was trapped. Some of the girls held the door closed. Then they stood on the toilet seats in the adjoining cubicles and threw bits of lighted notebook paper in on me. The most difficult thing is to go through the process of adjusting to what people will do to you. At first, I was frozen, sitting there wanting to cry and call for help. But there was no human help; my only help would come from God. I dug deep inside to find my well of energy and answers to get past the self-pity and turn it into action. I realized that God would rescue me, but I must act. I could not simply sit down and cry. I was no longer a child. I had to get past the fire and smoke that covered me. I had to put fear in its place. I returned the fire by throwing the paper back on my attackers.

Still, I was constantly bothered by name-calling and the anticipation of what brutal act was to come next. Even on those days when I was attacked many times during and between classes, I thought I must have the strength to complete the task. I pondered how to stop being the target, the wounded one. The Quakers had instructed us not to give our attackers the satisfaction of seeing the wounds they inflicted. I began to ignore my attackers, not weep inside when called names and sprayed with curse words. Instead, I got busy scheming how I could overcome them if given the chance, without risking my goal. I said a prayer that God would guide me in doing what was appropriate to defend myself.

Over and over again, Grandmother would remind me that I was one with God and therefore part of His infinite plan. She promised that when I fully understood that concept, I would realize my own value. I would know for certain I was equal, no matter what other people thought.

Meanwhile, I had to face the fact that I was surrounded by hostility, even in my own community. Increasingly, my people were losing their jobs and the privileges they had, such as donations of Christmas toys, food, used clothing, and furniture. White supremacists were pressuring our people to insist we nine give up. African Americans did not fully realize what they stood to lose in the future if we gave up—future rights to better education and better jobs.

People in my own church began asking me, "Why go where you're not welcome?" Stunned by the question, I would stop to ponder. Finally, I remembered the answer Grandmother had given me long ago when we both were listening on the radio to Jackie Robinson take his place on the baseball field in New York as the first African American to play in major league baseball. People booed, and I worried they would hurt him and asked Grandma why he wanted to be there where he was unwelcome. She replied, "If you go only where you are welcome, that's where other people want you to go, not where you choose to go. You're limited by their vision—not living your own dreams."

Now I was going where I was not welcome. When I spoke to Grandma about it, she said, "No one has the right to keep any institution we pay for with our own tax money from you. Central High is your school as much as theirs. Both your parents pay taxes."

The bullying continued. Some students called me ugly, stupid, and many other names that conjured up negative images in my mind. I had to adopt a sizable program in self-talk in order to rescue myself. My decision was to be in touch with my growing warrior deep inside. First I had to turn my cheek. I had to find a practical way of deflecting the names hurled toward me—a shield that would insulate my soul and keep me practicing peace and nonviolence. Above all else, I had to resist any response to the violence.

When someone called me stupid, my inner voice whispered, *Melba, they are strangers. What do they really know about you? You are brilliant. Look at your great grades throughout elementary and high school—always A's. Your grandma reads Shakespeare to you, and your mom has already earned a master's degree. She is studying for a doctorate. What do the bullies know of your family or what they have taught you?* Slowly, I could feel my determination to finish another day inside Central. I could feel my warrior deep inside me preparing to fight for what I deserved, to conquer the bullies and claim Central High as my own. All I needed was to be left in peace to learn so that I could graduate.

"You are so ugly, an ugly black nigger," the bullies would often shout. I looked up the word *nigger* in the dictionary and wrote that definition on paper. I found that no part of it fit my truth. My inner voice replied, *You have a great ponytail and a cute smile. You're beautiful, Melba. God has your picture on His fridge, remember. He celebrates your beauty each day. He celebrates your smart brain.*

Withstanding the day-to-day torture over the months was a tedious task. We could see little improvement; the bullies instead got more sophisticated—more skilled at their torturous acts. The sameness of the days and the rigors of repeated insults became a major hurdle. They seemed never ending. On some day, only long, deep, and continuous prayers helped me survive. The imprisonment over the weekends added to my sadness. It became hard to imagine that the year would end and I would again be free to be me.

For every insulting name I was called, I repeated the 23rd Psalm and spoke five positive compliments to myself. I discovered that the notion of self-talk requires surrender to the idea that God is a just God and that, inevitably, you will receive the very reward you seek or one even better than you might be striving for. Patience is the answer. I was learning to "wait on the Lord."

I sustained an inhuman number of mental and physical injuries from bullies surrounding me. Often I would respond by saying the Lord's Prayer aloud. But time after time, I reached for the inner voice that comforted me: *If I surrender to bullying torture, then they will use it as a tool against me and my community over and over again to hold on to their traditions of prejudice. They will deny me the vote, education, jobs, or housing. I will overcome their efforts by not falling victim to bullying.* At that point, my warrior roared inside. I felt totally determined to remain in Central High. It was my place as much as it was theirs. God had called me to this task to be present at Central High for a reason, and I could not give in to "sticks and stones."

As November turned into Thanksgiving, the 101st soldiers left us to our own devices. There was no official announcement. They were simply gone, replaced by the sloppy, dirty, giggling Arkansas state troopers. This change frightened me at first, but I was so much stronger now, having witnessed the discipline of the 101st and listened to Grandmother and my bodyguard. I was certain that I could count on God to give me the stamina to survive.

It became a bit more difficult to sustain myself after one of our nine was expelled from school for retaliation. Minnijean had been expelled after five months for dumping soup on a predator's head, even as he was in the midst of torturing her. The shouts in the hallways during class change became, "One down, eight to go." The more they shouted, the more determined I became to stay. Observing the bullies' joyous behavior at our mishap caused me to remember what Grandmother had said. They would be even more overjoyed if I committed suicide. From that point on, the more hostile their behavior, the more my warrior locked in my will to outwit and overcome their wrath. I did just that. With God's help, I completed the year.

Year after year as I grew older and witnessed the toppling of the walls of segregation at Little Rock and schools across the South, I began to understand the impact of my decision to remain at Central. Just as Dr. King had said, integrating Central wasn't all about me. It was about the opportunities future generations could claim based on my job. As Grandmother had said, "It was God's assignment." I became more and more grateful for not only my growing faith in God but also my trust that He would see me through all the challenges of my life, as He did that year in Central High.

—————

Christ was never a wimp. The Bible records His actions as purposeful, determined, energetic, and accountable.

Six

KEEPING MY FAITH
IN MY DARKEST HOUR

At age sixteen, during the summer of 1958, my adventures took me far beyond my imagination. On a tour sponsored by the NAACP, we nine spoke in eleven cities across the country. We toured state capitals and landmarks, including the United Nations, the White House, and all the Capitol buildings. We even went to a Johnny Mathis concert as his personal guests with VIP seats. All the while, we stayed in fancy hotels with outrageous room service, rode in shiny limousines, appeared on television and radio, and did newspaper interviews.

Integrating Central High had been a nightmare, but this tour was like a big dream, especially when the white doorman in front of the fancy New York hotel opened the door of the shiny limousine and said, "Won't you please step in, Miss," and bowed to me. I had to ask myself, "Was this Melba, with people standing in line for her autograph?"

Once I returned home, however, reality hit me with a shower of dark clouds. Governor Faubus had built a private high school for all the white students who once attended Central High School and closed all the public high schools across the city, including the African American high schools. But while others worried that the closing of Central High would bring integration to a screeching halt, I was distressed by Grandma's fast deterioration.

When Grandmother India first became ill, although she said it was nothing but a sore throat, I knew it was worse, much worse because she began to take naps during the day. She never took naps unless she was not feeling well at all. She had always said, "A body shouldn't take rest during daylight when there's God's work left to be done." Grandma refused to see the doctor for sniffling. "Just getting a little sniffle—no need to disturb the doc." After two weeks, Mother sent for our family doctor, who came and went away telling Mother that Grandma needed a specialist. We were all puzzled. He said he would send back a specialist to confirm and explain the diagnosis.

I grew even more nervous while waiting the few days it took for the white specialist from the University of Arkansas to come to the house to tell us what was really wrong with Grandma. Finally, one afternoon as she lay taking a nap, a white doctor, a throat specialist sent by our doctor, knocked on the door. He smiled as he entered the living room greeting all three of us, Mother, Conrad, and me. He introduced himself as Dr. Roth. I was impressed with the respect he showed to us.

Mother explained about Grandma's throat and how listless she seemed to be. He entered her room to examine her. I peeked through the crack in the door as he introduced himself to her, saying he'd heard about her stubborn cold and that he came to halt it before she infected all of us. I was pleased that he took a moment to tease Grandma, because that meant he saw her as a person. He smiled at her as he examined her body thoroughly and asked questions. He laughed with her, and when he laughed, he had kind eyes. And he also called her Miss India, not Aintee or by her first name as most white people did when they wanted to show disrespect for her age.

The doctor continued chitchatting with Grandma, charming her into allowing his examination. I satisfied myself that he seemed to be a nice man and would care for her, so I stepped into the living room to wait with Mother and Conrad. None of us spoke. I could hear the clock ticking the minutes away. After a long while, my stomach grew queasy, and my heart started pounding in my ears. I could almost hear the anxiousness that was overtaking us. I headed out the back door to sit awhile in the yard. But I couldn't sit still, so back and forth I paced—waiting and praying.

When Dr. Roth called Mother into the front hall, I rushed to stand by her side. The expression on his face was so serious, I couldn't make myself stay to hear what he had to say. Instead, I ran out the back door in tears and seated myself on the bottom step.

"You better get inside," my little brother, Conrad, said when he came out to get me after what felt like an eternity. "Something's wrong. Mother's crying out loud."

Mother Lois appeared pale and drawn. Her hands were shaking as she entered the living room. She was silent as she slumped down into the big, green velvet chair, tears streaming down her face.

"How long will it take her to get well?" Conrad asked.

"What's the matter with her?" I asked.

"It is leukemia," Mother whispered and stared at me with the most awful look in her eyes. Conrad suddenly left the room, not knowing what that was but knowing it was awful. Maybe he was too young to hear the truth. I did not call him back.

A week later, Grandma completely lost her sweet, gentle voice that had so many times whispered "I love you" as she tucked me into bed or served me lunch or walked with me to church. She could only write notes to me on paper. "Smile," she would write. "Smile because God is loving you and me both at this very moment." I would smile and then take a break outside to cry.

Day after day, I sat at the end of her bed reading the 23rd and 91st Psalms to her. On October 17, the ambulance carried her off to the hospital. We walked those shadowy, stark white halls as nurses in starched uniforms rustled back and forth. Whenever I entered her room, she forced a smile and pulled the headscarf down over the undyed gray hair that framed her weary face. The light in her eyes was dimming. On October 24, just before dawn the shriek of the ringing telephone awakened us all at once; we were called to the hospital. An unfamiliar, stoic-faced white doctor gathered us into a sterile, shiny, and windowless room to say the words— Grandmother India had expired.

"Expired—what does that mean?" Conrad asked.

"Died," the doctor said with no emotion in his voice.

Suddenly, Conrad broke away and ran down the hallway toward her room, shouting her name at the top of his lungs.

At that moment, I felt all life drain out of my body. I stood frozen. It felt like the walls, the floor, Mother, the doctor standing in front of me all caved into me. I could neither hear, see, nor feel anything around me. I couldn't catch my breath. It was utterly silent in the room. Had I died with her? Would she please let me die with her? I couldn't stand the thought of her leaving me.

I don't remember how we gathered up Conrad and got home, but I found myself sitting on the back stairs later that morning. There was nothing inside me telling me what I should do next. Grandma had been with me all my life. She was my playmate as a toddler, my home teacher as a preschooler, and always my friend whenever I needed her. She had taught me to read using the Bible, to grow plants, to clean toilets, to iron shirt collars, and always to be certain of God's love and to share it with others.

Grandma India had tucked me into bed almost every night of my sixteen years on earth. She had gotten down on her knees beside me to help me pray and make God my friend. Each morning, she had opened my bedroom drapes and welcomed the light to start my day. She was the safety in my darkness. She was music and sunlight, all my Sunday picnics, my Christmases, Easters, and birthdays. She was everything right and good that I knew of life.

Without her beside me, I would not have made it through the year at Central High to achieve the goal of integration. I was certain the sky would fall and there would be no tomorrow. Surely the sun would cease to shine. She was the hope and strength that had carried me. How could I go on without her?

Mother Lois and other arriving relatives called me to come inside, but only the chill of dusk drove me in. I heard people coming and going, footsteps echoing in the front of the house. Some of them brushed past or spoke to me, but I could not discern their words or speak back to them. I went directly to the bathroom, slammed the door, and stared into the mirror, wondering how my reflection could be there with Grandma India gone.

Later that evening, Mother Lois collapsed and the doctor had to be called to give her a sedative and put her to bed. Conrad whispered endlessly as though talking to Grandma could bring her back. I sat paralyzed and silent in the living room in the green chair that no longer felt like a cozy friend hugging me but instead a container for my rage—a collection of my doubts and calls for help from the Lord Jesus.

Church people came to take care of us. All their hot plates of food, tears, and talk about Grandma's wonderful character did not make my hurt go away. I felt empty and cold inside even when I stood by the fire. I would never feel her hug or love again. When bedtime came those first nights without her, I lay down to sleep on top of the covers with all my clothes on and prayed that Grandma India would come roust me up, order me to get into my pj's, and tuck me into bed. When she hadn't come by dawn, I stood and went back to the green chair to sit. In my diary, I wrote:

India Anette Peyton, India Anette Peyton, India Anette Peyton, India Anette Peyton, India Anette Peyton . . .

over and over again, until I filled two pages. Then I wrote:

God, I'm so angry at you. How could you take away the person I love most on the earth? India Anette Peyton.

70

I didn't move, not to eat or even to go to the bathroom, until late that afternoon when the pastor's wife dragged me up to wash my face.

"Cleanliness is next to godliness," she said sounding like Grandma India. That night, I went to bed in the same clothes and waited for Grandma to order me to change clothes and then tuck me in.

Early next morning, the third day without Grandma, Mother Lois, Conrad, and I found ourselves alone, sitting in the living room without the well-meaning friends. The house was in disarray, something Grandma India would never have tolerated. I stared at the mess, wondering who would come along and organize things. I could hear her melodic voice echo in my head: "Get off your 'sit-down' and show that you can get started doing His will. That's all God requires of you, and He will do the rest." I got up and started humming the spiritual I had heard her hum all my life, "I Am on the Battlefield for My Lord," as I tidied up and put things away in the places she always had. In the bathroom, I opened the window and screamed, "How I do hate you, God. Where are you?"

I made breakfast the way I had seen her do a million mornings, with napkins and placemats and silverware sparkling. As the toaster purred, I was careful to follow Grandmother's instructions about fallen egg yolks. Mine stood like soldiers on parade. *She would have been proud of me*, I thought, as I called Conrad and Mother Lois into the kitchen. They were surprised and pleased.

As we took our seats around the table, we all stared at the empty fourth chair—her chair. We couldn't hold back the tears. I could just hear Grandma laughing as she teased us, "Tear-soaked eggs and toast, you ought to be ashamed." Despite the fact that I didn't remember ever having a family meal without her, we got through that first meal somehow. I couldn't stop staring at her empty chair and the unused place setting, as though wishing it would bring her back.

The day of Grandma India's funeral, I got up early to clean and scrub the house—even the toilets—to make certain everything was just as Grandma would have it. I was sweeping off the front steps when the long, black, shiny limousine, just like the ones I had ridden in while in New York, pulled up in front of the house. I didn't want to ride in that long, black car to the church with all my crying relatives. I didn't want to see them load up Grandma India at the church to go on her last ride to the cemetery. I ran inside and slammed the front door.

I knew I should be getting dressed to go to our church for Grandma India's funeral, but something inside was holding me back. I couldn't make myself go with Mother, Conrad, and the other relatives and church members to do that awful thing: to sit in church looking at Grandma India stiff and cold, lying so still in a wooden box, and then to bury her. How could I stand still watching strangers shovel dirt over her wooden box? While neighbors and friends arrived at our house in their Sunday clothing, I wore jeans and a loose shirt and had uncombed hair. People stared at me, but I said nothing.

I would leave my room to see what was going on, then duck back in and slam the door. Hard. Then I crept down the hall to Mama Lois's bedroom to watch the sisters from Grandma's church in North Little Rock help her put on the white wool dress she had for the funeral. I looked into her eyes and said nothing and walked back into my room.

Suddenly, my aunt Mae came and banged on the door to my room. "You better come out here, girl. You better get yourself together." Miss Lela Brown from our church was with her shouting, "You look a might undone in them jeans." I did not answer. I could hear the chatter in the living room where the minister was gathered with other people, starting to say a prayer aloud. I stepped down the hall to join them and paused.

At that moment, they hushed up and stared at me as if I were some awful criminal. Once again, several of the women came toward me with their hands outstretched, saying how much Grandma loved me—as if I didn't already know that. "You can't let her go alone—she needs you. If you really love someone, you go all the way with them, all the way to the grave."

"I don't know what you're doing, Melba Joy, but you know you gotta get dressed. Now you hurry. You can't hold up everything," Aintee Mae said, standing there in her Sunday white, pointing her finger at me. "You've got to walk this last mile with your grandmother."

I walked down the hall toward the living room, thinking for an instant that maybe they all were right; if I went with them to bury Grandma, it might not be so bad. But then I felt something deep inside. I squeezed my eyes tight and put my hands over my ears. I was standing motionless in the hallway with my aunt behind me, trying to push me forward. Some man whom I didn't even know was also telling me what to do. He kept saying my grandma was dead. *Shut up*, I thought to myself. *Grandma India would never, never die and leave me*. I felt my entire body start to tremble, a trembling that got stronger and stronger as I fought against it.

That's when a voice screamed so loud it hurt my throat and my ears. "*Grandma is not dead!*" It was an angry voice that sounded much like my own. "There is no funeral to go to! Shut up!"

"It's all right, Melba . . . I understand." Mother Lois stood over me speaking in a calm voice, tears running down her face. She was treating me as if something was wrong with me.

"Never mind, I'll tend to her." I heard the familiar tones of our family doctor, then felt a needle prick in my arm. The shot did its job—all of my being softened into an indefinable drift to nowhere. Sometime later, when I became conscious, I was sitting in the big, green chair from the living room, which had been moved into my bedroom. There was only silence around me. The house seemed empty. I folded my arms against the chill, feeling even more lonely and lost than before. Then I heard two church ladies' voices in the kitchen and the sound of rattling dishes, but it still felt as if I were alone.

I walked into Grandma India's room where she kept all her personal belongings, special items she called her "dibbies." I reached out to stroke her embroidered pillow that read, "God is love." Then I drew my hand back as though she would catch me. It had been one of her untouchables. Now I could touch her dibbies all I wanted because she wasn't there to say no.

I would have given anything to have her slap my hand as I picked up her green music box with the ivory cameo figure on top and held it to my chest. It was her favorite possession. When I lifted the lid, it played "Stardust." The tinny music filled the air as I opened the door to her closet. There hung all her clothes. I could smell the scent of vanilla flavoring she had made her special perfume. I touched her blue crepe dress with the buttons down the front. All her shawls hung across hangers, waiting for her to choose one.

I nuzzled among her clothes and hugged a bunch of her dresses that held her personal aroma. It made me feel as though she were hugging me. I didn't know where it came from, but a voice seemed to say to me that she loved me just the same, even though I could no longer see her. I stood still for a long time, feeling her all around me.

After a week's recuperation, during which I stayed in my locked room, Mother Lois and Conrad went back to their schools. Central High and all the African American high schools remained closed to halt integration. I had no place to go. Governor Faubus had won this round. Neither the Supreme Court justices, nor the president, nor the NAACP, nor anybody else could stop him. The white people had built a huge private school, open only to their chosen ones.

I was left alone in that house with Grandma's memories all around me. At first, I thought I would lose my mind. I wanted more than anything to see her as she was, alive and well, to speak with her just once more. Sure enough, just as clear as a bell, one afternoon I heard Grandma's voice remind me that I couldn't lose my mind because God inhabited my mind. One day melted into another the way they do when you don't have a place you belong or a work routine. I didn't follow any pattern in eating or bathing or dressing or any of the other tasks I had to do to live. I felt numb and cold, like a statue. It was as though I lived behind a big piece of glass that separated me from all other living people. I was waiting for someone or something to rescue me. I wanted the God I had abandoned to prove to me that He did care for me, even though I hated Him. I picked up Grandmother's tattered Bible and began reading the psalms. I read for two hours before I realized I felt better. I stood up to take care of some personal hygiene. Peace washed over me with the bath water.

A few nights later, Grandma India came to me in a dream that was so real I felt as though I could reach out and touch her. She was robust and smiling. "Life is a precious gift, my child—a cherished grant only to those who use it to the fullest each day," she said as she hugged me and smiled. "Do not squander God's gift."

The next morning, I sat straight upright, feeling as though she were nearby. Then I remembered she couldn't be, and I was a bundle of sadness again. Still, I felt a rush of new energy. I knew I had to resume my morning studies and afternoon housework. I felt her watching me. So with the television playing in the background to lessen my loneliness, I began doing all the household chores. I discovered the busier I kept myself, the better I felt. Deep inside I knew for certain no one was going to rescue me. I had to renew my relationship with God—I had to trust again in order to let Him rescue me.

As the school year rolled deeper into winter, the governor's closing of our schools continued to be challenged by US authority. At first, President Eisenhower expressed hope that public sentiment would force the governor to reopen public schools. But with the creation of private schools for whites only, based on the school board's and the superintendent of schools' plan to limit integration, whites were indeed able to run their private schools without tax money.

The NAACP told us five who remained to integrate Central High to continue to wait, that the case hinged on our not registering in another school. So wait we did, while newspapers reported that the segregationists hoped we'd either register at another school or, better yet, be killed.

Those annoying, threatening nighttime calls continued. But they came without the emotional paralysis that came from losing Grandma India. I just answered them by repeating the 23rd Psalm and slamming the phone down. I no longer feared the callers because the pain of Grandma's loss outweighed everything else.

Life seemed to be happening as though I were a robot on automatic pilot. The approach of Christmas gave me an opportunity to make myself very busy. Mother Lois had little time to shop and cook and decorate. Somehow, I felt obligated to keep the house running the way Grandma wanted it. I found myself taking on her role, becoming more and more like her every day. I made a list of all the things I remembered she had done in holiday seasons past and then completed everything on that list. Listening to carols and decorating the Christmas tree, we even laughed when Conrad did his Santa routine. Still, there were no gingerbread men with jelly bean eyes or double butter cakes because none of us knew the recipes.

Worst of all, we forgot to hang stockings. Grandma India always hung the stockings and filled them with tiny goodies from Santa, like a bracelet and toothpaste and warm socks that she had knitted. On Christmas Day I sat alone, trying to remember just what it was like to have her present. All our family members had gathered as usual. Except for Mother, they laughed louder and sang louder, pretending everything was joyous. They never even asked why I sat alone staring out the window.

Grandma India had always said that if a body has faith, even if it is only the size of a mustard seed, the promise of spring would renew all things, and so it was with me. I felt her energy driving me to be a part of the rebirth. By March of 1959, I actually began to relish my days filled with housework, studying, and watching soap operas. I was no longer angry at God. I realized God did not take Grandma to punish me. Could it be that He took her to reward her for her good deeds? God loves me and is always there for me even when I abandon Him. Grandma wanted me to claim life at its fullest, and so that is exactly what I determined to do. Someway, somehow I was going to get myself back into school.

God is there for us even when we are angry with Him. Faith and trust in God are the only way to survive. Faith can be renewed, if we are willing to surrender. With renewal comes hope for healing and the ability to move forward.

Seven

GOD IS EVERYWHERE, ESPECIALLY IN CALIFORNIA

Somehow a threat to your life makes you much more aware of a need for Jesus. That's the time when you feel abandoned, and you want something or somebody to hold on to. The first thing you realize is that no human being can fulfill that spot.

A year later, by the end of the 1959 school semester, three of our number had already moved to other cities to attend school. It became clear over that winter that all of us would have to escape to the North to save our lives. The Ku Klux Klan bullies had posted flyers all over town with "$10,000 if dead, $5,000 alive." Frequently, cars would drive by our house filled with gnarly looking white men who would point our way.

I found myself locked down and imprisoned by this Klan treatment. Because Governor Faubus had closed all Little Rock schools, I was asked by the NAACP not to enter another school so as to keep the court case open. I had spent a year at home alone and lonely, having to cope with reality including life-changing milestones, like the death of Grandma India. I began believing for a time that God had abandoned me.

I never thought I would be grateful to the Klan for any reason; however, yea team, those flyers and stalkers speeded up my ticket out of Little Rock. The NAACP and my parents took the threats seriously and told me that I would have to leave Arkansas to save my life. I was overjoyed. I was so bored spending all my time in the house or in the company of the adults guarding me. Each of the six of us still in Arkansas during the year following the integration of Central was placed with families across the United States. The NAACP put out urgent calls to members in branches across the country in order to solicit folks who would take in and protect and give a safe home to our members of the nine. I was off to California. I was set to complete my senior year of classes in a new place with strangers. Neither Mother nor I had met our sponsors, the Santa Rosa NAACP.

I immediately began daydreaming about my life with a wealthy African American family in California who would provide me with a telephone and subscriptions to *Ebony* and *Seventeen* magazines and a gorgeously decorated bedroom, tons of friends, and the redo of the prom I had missed. Of course, I envisioned a very comfortable African American family who lived in a moderate-sized mansion like the ones I had seen on television shows about Californians. Maybe when I turned eighteen they could afford to give me a used car. I pushed the dream as far as I could expand it.

When I was told I would be met by members of the Santa Rosa, California, NAACP at the San Francisco airport, I was comfortable and excited. "Praise God," I whispered as I stood in the vast, unfamiliar airport, feeling lost in a strange city that I knew nothing about. I was stunned when a group of fifteen or so white adult folks rushed up to greet me and reached out to hug me. White people didn't hug us. What was wrong with these smiling, kind-voiced people? It was frightening. What did they want?

I hoped the NAACP committee of African Americans was nearby to rescue me. I didn't know what to say when those white people introduced themselves as NAACP members. My mind was on fire wondering if they were really members of the Ku Klux Klan, coming to get rid of me so they could collect the $10,000. Only the trust that God couldn't bring me all this far and drop me consoled me momentarily. I had no choice in that huge, unfamiliar city but to trust God and go with them as they loaded me in a van to take me to the family I'd be living with. I did not know what else to do.

No one in the NAACP of Arkansas or the national group had told me that my hosts or my family might be white. En route to Santa Rosa, I was questioning myself about what got me into this mess. Were the people I was riding with really a welcoming NAACP team? Were they taking me to meet an African American family? Finally, we turned into a long, gravelly driveway that crunched under tires as we rode onto the farm. Ahead was a two-story, white farmhouse with a range of vast, green mountains looming in the distance and an occasional cow roaming about. The peaked roof covered a number of small loft rooms. We parked and got out of the van.

Suddenly, I was introduced to the family I would be living with. I was astonished and frightened to find that they were white. Mrs. McCabe told me to call her Kay and invited me and the committee members to come inside. There I met the two smallest members of the family and was told that there were two other children my age who were still at school. Then Kay told me, "My husband, George, will be home soon. He's teaching a psychology class at San Francisco State today."

It was warm and rustic inside the house, with chunky furniture, well-worn hardwood floors, and embroidered and crocheted pillows. The aroma of beef stew hung in the air. Beyond the kitchen in the backyard were pigs, goats, and the cows to be milked. Although Kay said I was welcome, I didn't feel welcome in a white stranger's home. I thought NAACP meant black.

The McCabes were as welcoming, kind, and soft-spoken as they could be. However, the only words to describe my feelings were frightened beyond comprehension. Their neighbors had thrown rocks at me in front of the house upon my arrival. When Dr. George McCabe arrived home, he picked up the rocks and threw them back, saying it was none of their business.

With their reddish hair and hazel eyes, the McCabes resembled the people in the Little Rock mob who had chased me from Central High in 1957. The adults, Kay, a petite woman with copper-brown bangs that lay across her forehead and tortoiseshell glasses, and George, a tall and lanky six-feet-two bony man with flaming red hair and blue eyes, resembled closely the predators I feared. The sisters, especially the two older ones, one my age and one a year younger, resembled the students of Central High who had defined the word *misery* for me by making it my reality.

Instead of magazine subscriptions and a glamorous room all to myself, I was to share a bedroom with two white teenage strangers on an isolated farm in Santa Rosa, California, in the most modest of circumstances. I was surrounded by an ordinary neighborhood of farmers, ordinary houses, farm animals, and a way of life I knew absolutely nothing about. I was particularly unnerved by the group of cows that gathered in a neat row at a fence just outside my bedroom window. They peered in at me as I squealed and stared back at them, wondering why they were there. No one had explained that their feeding trough was there. They had gathered for their meal. I prayed so hard and spent many sleepless hours face down in my pillow crying that first week. What was I doing there with those white people? I was both afraid and lonely—I was on pins and needles, waiting for something to go wrong. I didn't tell Mom anything about being miserable. I didn't want to go back to Little Rock. Besides, I didn't want to worry her. I told myself that after two awful years of fright, I deserved peace and pleasure. I deserved to be with loving people who would take care of me. The answer came back, what if that is exactly what you have here? What if these are the loving people you asked God for? Day after day, moment after moment, they taught me the meaning of kindness, acceptance, and love. There was not one iota of evidence that they wished to harm me in any way.

Both George and Kay escorted me to school for registration. They were gentle in making certain that I was comfortable and set for the right classes. They introduced me to the principal and his assistant and then turned me over to my new sisters, Joanie, age fifteen, and Judy, sixteen. Joanie and Judy escorted me from class to class, casually introducing me to their friends without any prologue (like explaining where I came from or what I was doing there). Because of all the inquiries of the press and calls to have me speak, George said I should use my middle name, thus abandoning my identification as a civil rights heroine, one of the Little Rock Nine.

George decided I would not speak or give interviews. "You will have the opportunity here to become a regular high school senior, free of all that confusion. I want you to relax and enjoy yourself." Enjoy—the word echoed in my ear. My mother had never used that word before. *What would it be like to feel joy?* I wondered. I could not relax. Once again, I was an African American alone among hundreds of white students. Montgomery High School was small, well equipped, and warmly decorated. However, there were only four other African Americans attending, and I seldom saw them. Sometimes I had to remind myself that I was not back at Central High as I moved among a sea of white faces. The big differences were that some of them smiled and no one reached out to hit me.

From the first day I arrived to my classes, not one of those white students called me a name, made rude gestures, or behaved in any way unwelcoming to me. Instead, many of them wore sweet facial expressions and smiled at me as they opened doors for me, picked up my dropped books, and directed me to my next class. To my amazement, the end of the first week came, and I found myself packed into a car owned by a student named Mary on my way to the Pickup Drive-In to get a hamburger. And yes, I did have a fleeting thought that they would take me to the woods, tie me up, and leave me there or hang me. It didn't happen.

After school, they dropped me off at home so that I could relax. Time after time, I exhausted myself waiting for abuse, dreaming up ugly things that could happen to me. The Mc-

Cabes treated me as family—billeting me in the room with Judy and Joanie. The two younger children, Ricky and Dori, had their own rooms.

The McCabes consistently showed me their compassion. When the local swimming pool refused to allow me to swim, George gathered his university friends and marched in front of the pool to protest, chanting as they held large placards. After one day, the manager called to say I would be allowed to swim.

I asked the McCabes if I could become a member of their church family. I told them that I had been Methodist. As they were Quakers, they suggested I go to another church across town. After a couple of visits, I determined I was the only person of color in that church, which was a little uncomfortable for me. I asked George if he knew where all the black people were. He said there were only about seven African American adults and seven young people in the town, with only two of those attending my high school. I went back to the white church and stayed there and was befriended.

As time passed, Kay McCabe became someone I could talk to. She listened quietly without judgment—never criticizing me or making me feel less valuable. I began to feel she honestly liked me. When I came home complaining that my unfashionable Southern clothes made me stand out, she took money from the cookie jar to buy me a decent skirt and sweater.

Ultimately, as time passed, George determined there were no African Americans nearby for me to date. So he launched a campaign to find one. He went to several junior colleges and colleges to interview their basketball teams. I was so embarrassed, besides which, I felt I was sinning as Grandma had said I couldn't date until I was eighteen. Nevertheless, I felt his compassion and willingness to do whatever necessary to keep me from being alone and without a social life.

With time, I would learn that God is everywhere, especially in California. His love exists without limitations of color or race. He certainly was present in the love-filled McCabe home. The love and care given me by George and Kay McCabe, and each and every member of their family, never wavered or caused me one moment of physical or mental pain. Their attitudes toward me expanded my horizons and taught me about unprejudiced white people outside of Little Rock and the meaning of unconditional love.

Their very special acceptance and love would become a life-changing experience for me. They would remain my primary family throughout my life until this very moment. Living with the McCabes and being welcomed so completely by them also would initiate a major shift in my perception of my place in the world and my sense of humanity.

The comfort and sense of freedom they provided gave me a sense of domain and self-confidence in the public arena. Being with them took away the power and sway white people had held over me for all of my life spent in Arkansas. Now I understood the Constitution—we are all equal and born entitled to equal rights. Only sometimes it does not work out. Folks of color aren't granted privilege and rights—they have to fight for them and claim them deep inside.

Until that moment, I had always accorded freedom with being white—only white people were truly free, I had thought while living in Arkansas. Now the McCabes taught me that *white*, a word I had often substituted for freedom, was a state of mind, and *freedom* was mine to choose. It was my decision to choose to be free and to not be limited by negative behavior and the attitudes of racists.

George and Kay McCabe became parents to me. I would later come to understand that even before I arrived, they had been activists. It was Mom McCabe who had helped to create the local branch of the NAACP, the Quaker church, and the local PBS television station; marched for voters' rights; and created preschools and a widely acclaimed, statewide Russian River project celebrated for seven days each year. She served her community based on her belief that everyone is equal with strength, courage, faith, and the freedom to dream. She endowed me with some of that same spirit.

The McCabes helped me transition to college—first Santa Rosa Junior College and then San Francisco State University. It was the experience of living with them that allowed me to seek jobs where none of my people worked and climb other uncharted professional mountains without the primal fear of whites that I had lived with all my life. Now they were just people—people like me, like Mom and Dad McCabe.

Since my first consciousness of being African American, of being alive, I had struggled with the notion of being equal, feeling equal. After interacting with the McCabes, much of that was erased or put into context. They were white, educated, brilliant, and kind, but they were just people, just like the African American people I knew. Never for an instant had they caused me to feel less valuable, less than equal in any way. To the contrary, they treated me as though I were precious royalty—one of their own children to be cherished.

Life's lessons come from unexpected places. We cannot afford to allow prejudices to shut out God's blessings. Being equal is based on seeing equal. It is seated in each individual's willingness to claim their own equality despite all evidence to the contrary and all talk by others who dare to question their value.

Eight

I Didn't Expect It
to Happen This Way

When I was growing up in the 1950s in Little Rock, Arkansas, no one talked to me about romantic love relationships of any description. The only thing I could see in front of me was that my father and mother never got along, and it made for a very explosive lifestyle, particularly amid the threats and oppression of the Klan and all the whites around me. There was disagreement in my family. By the time I was five, they were divorcing. When I was nine, they were still in court bickering over custody of my brother and me.

When I visited some of my friends, I could see that they had mothers and fathers who loved each other. They had fathers they could count on to hold their hand, take them to the park, and sit with them in church. For most of my life, I had only my grandmother and my mother.

While living in California with the McCabes, I became accustomed to being in the presence of white people. I knew that, unlike the awful racists in Little Rock, there were some kind white people.

Seldom did I think about dating or having a boyfriend. When I did, I heard the voices of my mother and grandmother admonishing me that I shouldn't have those thoughts until age eighteen.

At age nineteen and living on my own in an apartment with a roommate while attending San Francisco State University, I was at a loss to understand all of the new Northern lifestyle I had been cast into. Still, I knew there was no dating across the lines, and I never had a longing for a date with a white man. When friends brought home a date for my roommate, and he started talking to me instead, the only thing I noticed about him was that he was white and a soldier wearing a green uniform. He resembled one of the 101st Airborne soldiers who had guarded me in Little Rock.

This man, whom I will call Jay, was more persistent with each visit. At the time, my roommate was dating someone else and said to me, "Go ahead, go out with him. What difference does it make?" I said it was something I absolutely couldn't do, simply because it just wasn't appropriate according to my Southern upbringing. I knew my grandmother and mother would have a fit.

On Saturday morning a week later, when my roommate was out of town, Jay knocked on my door. I told him that Mary wasn't home, and he said, "I didn't come to see Mary. I came to see you. Come on, let's grab some breakfast and go to the park."

"No, thank you," I replied. "Mary will be back tomorrow."

"I'm not waiting for Mary. I'm waiting for you."

"I don't date white men. It's early, and I'm going back to bed," I said as I began pushing the door closed.

"I didn't say anything about dating. I just said I want to have a bite of breakfast and go for a walk in the park."

"As I said, I don't date white men. Sorry, I have to go back to bed. Saturday is my only day to sleep in." I shut the door hoping he would go away.

As I laid my head on the pillow, the only thing I thought was that he had the most interesting opal-green eyes, almost the same color as his uniform. Was he anything like the 101st soldiers who had guarded me, and what would it be like to talk to him about ordinary things?

The blast of the alarm awakened me at 10:00 a.m. I circled around the apartment, putting on the teapot and looking for cornflakes. Once again, the doorbell rang. I answered the door and, sure enough, there he was with the same green eyes, the same smile, the same freckles and red hair.

"Okay," he said. "Nap over. Ready to get going?"

"I don't date white men."

"I didn't say anything about a date. You have to eat somewhere. Why not come eat with me?" he said. "Do what you like. I'll be waiting here for you. If we can't have breakfast, maybe we can have dinner."

He sat down on the floor, picked up a magazine, and began to read. I stood there in my robe staring at him, thinking this white soldier would get me into trouble. I had such a difficult time renting the apartment because I was black. I was the only black person I had ever seen living on Sutter Street in downtown San Francisco. Even the neighborhood grocer asked where I came from, who I was, living in that neighborhood. The other people of color I saw were either sweeping the streets or cleaning the hotel across the street. So I thought to myself, *I need to do something to get rid of this guy before the landlady sees him hanging around the hall.* I quickly got dressed and pointed my way to the front door.

As we walked down the steep Sutter Street hill toward the center of downtown San Francisco, he grabbed my arm. "Okay now, be careful," he whispered in a caring tone. Whenever he spoke to me, the tone in his compassionate voice echoed in my head. We were silent for a block. He let go of my arm when we reached level ground. And I said, "We're going to get in trouble, you know. Where I come from, white men don't walk with black women."

"Where I come from, they do," he said. "Why can't you see me as a man? Why not stop thinking of the color of my skin?"

I didn't have another word to say because I didn't have an answer. The only thing I did know for certain was that I was so comfortable with him that I didn't want to leave. I knew somehow that he wasn't going to hurt me.

As we entered the restaurant, he told me it was a world-famous breakfast restaurant and asked if I'd ever had eggs Benedict.

"What's that?" I asked.

"Let me show you."

I was so nervous I could hear my heart pounding in my ear because I wondered if the waiter would seat us together. I had been away from Little Rock for almost two years now, but I still couldn't get rid of the notion that I was separate from white people and that there were Southern rules of behavior that would rear their ugly heads at some time or another. Jay held the chair for me as we were seated comfortably at a table. Jay put in the order for both of us: "Eggs Benedict."

His steely eyes caught mine over the table, and for a time I felt hypnotized, unable to look away.

"Where are you from?"

"Down South, Little Rock, Arkansas."

"You're a long way from home."

"I guess so."

"How did you get out here?"

All of a sudden, I heard words just pouring out of me like a gushing waterfall. Before I knew it, I had told him about my life in Little Rock, the explanation of my past, my fears, and the sorrow and sadness carried deep inside that weighed down my day. I talked to him about many things I hadn't told anyone, feelings I hadn't even known existed that were buried deep down inside. Perhaps it was the sympathetic look on his face or the way he occasionally stroked the back of my hand with his finger or his saying, "That's all over. You will never have to live that way again." Or maybe it was the tears that filled his huge eyes as I talked of Central High. Whatever the reason, I could not stop myself—even though I sounded out of control. Thankfully, midway through the meal, I had to make my way to the ladies' room. That silenced me.

I had waited as long as I could because I was frightened patrons would call me a name or disrespect me. Jay asked the waiter where the ladies' room was. My destination meant I had to squeeze through the tables and past lots of people. Oh, how I dreaded it.

"Fill this water pitcher please, and also I'd like more orange juice," a stranger's voice shouted at me. I didn't know what to do.

I said, "I'm not the waitress."

"Listen here, nigger, I said fill this pitcher and get me more orange juice," the man screeched aloud.

I looked at Jay across the room. His startled expression radiated real anger. He moved toward me with a swift thrust. Before he got there, the man said again even louder, "Didn't you hear me? Don't you speak English? Fill this pitcher and get me more orange juice now."

"Did you hear her? She's not the waitress," Jay said with anger in his voice and posture.

"Then what is she doing in here?" the other man shouted.

The man stood up with anger on his face, and he was all of the six feet two that Jay stood. Jay lunged at him and grabbed the front of his throat with an iron-firm claw. "Sorry that you have to leave." Then Jay began backing him toward the front door. "Don't worry about your bill. I'll take care of it." The woman who sat beside him looked aghast and followed him out the door.

"Okay, Ladybug, let's go." Jay took my hand and led me to the bathroom door, where he waited outside for me. By that time, I was in tears. When I stepped out of the ladies' room, he took my hand and guided me through the tables and people back to our table at the front of the restaurant with our unfinished eggs Benedict. I felt people's eyes on my back; I got nervous and wanted to quickly get out the door.

Jay said, "Take your time. We're not in a hurry."

He took out some money and paid our bill and asked about the other man's bill. The waiter told him not to worry—"You and your lady have a nice day."

Jay said, "Let's get some ice cream."

We stayed together for the rest of the day, walking the hills of downtown San Francisco, looking in shops, talking, and riding on cable cars. He spoke very little; I nervously talked a lot. His quiet voice, welcoming smile, and protective manner made me more comfortable and safer than I could ever remember being. I actually caught myself smiling.

"So this is what safety feels like," I whispered to God. "This must be what it's like to know that You are with me all the time and to trust that You are with me and that my safety does not depend on another human being."

After a block of silence, I asked him what he did in the army. He said he was a Specialist, an expert in martial arts and the kind of soldier who was dropped from a helicopter to survey the terrain and risks and location of enemy soldiers before the other US soldiers arrived. His strength, muscular stature, self-confident movement, and kind manner made me feel content. By the time we arrived back at my apartment, it was dark. Jay attempted to kiss me good night, and I did not resist him. Instead, I stepped on tippy toes and held him close, hoping he would hold me forever.

When I was alone in my apartment, I asked myself, "What am I doing? My Little Rock friends will hate me, my mother will think I had a nervous breakdown, and reporters will write a big, nasty news story about how one of the Little Rock Nine kissed a white guy who looked just like the men from the mob who chased her with hanging ropes." I felt guilty and swore I would never go out with him again. But I couldn't stop myself from spending time with him. I wanted more and more of the feeling he brought that warmed my insides, a feeling of safety and joy, a feeling of being wanted and of knowing that I was valuable to him.

The thing Jay provided to me that no one other than Kay McCabe had before was an opportunity to talk with another human being who listened and gave me their full attention. He listened to me forever, never displaying a bored or disapproving expression. He responded by squeezing my hand, moving to sit beside me, or putting his arm around me.

It was as though I had waited all my life to tell someone of my feelings of being afraid, of going to downtown Little Rock at Christmas with my five-year-old hopes to sit on Santa's lap and being rejected, or of facing the trauma of Central High haters. I spilled the pain and sadness of all that had happened to me when Grandma died and how much I hurt inside from always trying to stretch and not be seen as less than.

Jay always listened to me. In exchange, he told me of his almost-perfect life growing up on a perfect ranch in Washington with family all around and with perfect parents— a mother who canned, baked cakes and pies, and raised horses—and of being a boy whose life was filled with barrels of hope and joy. For the first time in my life, I was not lonely deep inside. Jay took me on a trip to Reno, Nevada, and suddenly before I knew what happened, we were married.

Life with Jay was something I didn't know how to define or accept. I had no experience with how to be a wife or how to be pregnant. Suddenly I had a stranger inside me who wanted to eat things I had never eaten before. I had no idea what happened during pregnancy. Jay did know as he had been around sisters who were pregnant.

Increasingly, I felt I was in a role on a movie screen, one I had not signed up for as I didn't know what was required. I had no one to talk to about all the strange feelings in my body. Mother was barely talking to me, of course, because I had married a white man without her permission. I prayed hard for some answers. All that came back was the knowledge that God was with me, and I should keep trusting Him.

I had to quickly learn how to cook. Day by day, I became more bored. My mother had been shocked when I told her what I had done. She told me I was at the wrong place at the wrong time. "You must go back and finish college; you must get your master's degree and your doctorate and follow the road to become a teacher or a lawyer."

Mother called me every single Sunday to tell me how disappointed she was. She repeated the lines, "Anybody could get married and anybody could get pregnant. If you are a black woman in this country, you must be educated." For the other six days of the week, as I washed the dishes or mopped the floors, I would be haunted by her words. Anybody can clean the house, make a bed, sweep the floor, or mop the kitchen, and someone would always come along and mess it up again. But read a book and get a degree, and it's yours forever.

To get out of the house, I took a job working for the federal government. When my white coworkers saw that my husband was white and I was carrying a baby, they asked, "How will this child grow up in the world? It will be mixed." For weeks on end, I worried about this. When I finally spoke to Jay about it, he replied, "Toward the sky. She will grow up toward the sky. She will be tall and graceful like you, my chocolate angel."

From the beginning, my pregnancy was difficult. By month four, doctors urged me to leave work and to enter the Army Presidio Hospital in San Francisco, where I remained until the baby was born. My days and nights were even more boring now. I was confined to bed rest. At least there I didn't feel so conspicuous because there were two other mixed couples, and we became acquainted with them.

When the time came for the baby's birth, I was in labor thirty-six hours. No one had told me what would happen during childbirth. The medical staff sent a special doctor down to help as I was having such difficulty. At one point, they called Mother to stand by to fly in to see me. I heard their hopeless whispers and prayed aloud around the clock through my awful pain.

After the birth, when the nurse came to bring my baby to me, she insisted on rereading both our tags because she thought she had the wrong mom. My daughter, Kellie, had green eyes and a porcelain complexion with reddish-brown hair. She said, "You can't be Melba Joy Beals, can you?" When I replied I was, she reluctantly handed me my baby.

Just before we left the hospital, the doctor took us aside and said, "If you are to remain healthy, do not have any more children for at least the next five years. To be frank, Mrs. Beals, I am not sure you should ever have any more children. There is a rumor afoot for whatever reason that black women are built in such a way that they find it easier to birth children. Mr. Beals, this black woman is not one of them; she almost died. You almost lost her. Please, do not get pregnant. Do not come back here."

From birth, my baby, Kellie, was a delight. Like her father, she was quiet but alert and sweet in her behavior. For a time, we lived in the same bliss that we had in our early months of marriage. Now I had what I always wanted—a family. I felt safe and protected. We lived in the Haight-Ashbury district, where we were deep in the revolution of the '60s. Social change was moving forward and boiling right in front of me.

A year passed, and being a wife and mother was just not enough for me. Although I attended church and prayed day and night, I felt restless and devalued. I could not handle the day-to-day routine of being isolated from friends with no projects, no homework, and no educational goals. I felt as though I were visiting a strange planet and not comfortable with anything around me. I loved my daughter, I loved and adored my husband, but it was not enough. I pleaded with my husband to allow me to go back to school to complete my bachelor's degree.

I began taking classes, and the more I focused on my education and new opportunities for women in society, the more I knew something needed to change. I believed I could be a good wife and mother and an educated, productive person at the same time. I wanted to have a career; I wanted to go to work each day. I wanted to march and challenge the rules that had governed women and wives up until then.

The more I talked about my need to have a career, the angrier my husband became. Jay wanted me to focus on improving my dinner recipes, folding the clothes more carefully, and exercising to keep the weight off. Above all else, he wanted me pregnant and more children, a male heir to carry on his military obsession.

Eventually, our conflict led to unhappy days and miserable evenings. I would come home from school excited about Kant's theories of philosophy, and Jay would watch television and ask me to please be quiet and get him a sandwich.

I tried hard to be the wife he wanted because I loved him, and I wanted to keep my family together. Daily I asked God to make me a good wife and to change Jay's vision into whatever it took for him to see me as a good wife. However, the more I did what he wanted, the more I felt I was shedding Melba and becoming someone I didn't know. Each week, Mother called to admonish me for not completing my college degree. She said, "Education lasts forever, but husbands are temporary."

I was watching the news seeing the march on Washington and the other civil rights actions going on. I wanted to join my colleagues, but instead I was home trying to conform to the duties that Jay felt were necessary in order to be a perfect wife. This man who in the beginning was my rescuer, my comfort, my joy, and my peace now seemed like my jailer.

I felt enslaved within the confines of his definition of marriage. I had no role model and no one to help me sort through my feelings. Of course, I had Sunday church people to talk with, but I could not tell all my secrets to strangers so I felt alone and confused. I prayed hard to God because I did not want to lose my family, and I could not lose myself.

Against Jay's desires, I went back to work at my job with the federal government. I remember coming home one day to find my baby gone, everything gone including the garbage. Just as I stretched out on the floor screaming, the phone rang. "I decided we needed to move. Let me give you our new address." Jay had moved us to another apartment. I was astounded that he would make such a decision without consulting me.

My first reaction was to call the minister of our church. I met with him the following day. He said that our conflict was one faced by many couples in these times of change. It was about the surrender of ego. My ego was in its infancy and growing while his was over the top. We needed to ask God for guidance to have a Christian marriage.

At the next meeting, Jay was present, and the minister tried to explain to him that I was not the same as when we came together. Then, I was very weak and worn down by my experiences in Little Rock and all the change since. He congratulated Jay for his kindness and told him that by his love and nurturing, he had refreshed my spirit and healed the wounds from that era of my life.

The minister then said, "This was your assigned task from God. You have shown Melba that all white people are not walking around with guns, ropes, and white sheets waiting to hang her. You have shown her genuine love and caring, and she understands that. You have to understand her work is not done here, and God will have more assignments for her as His warrior. You need to ask yourself how you will support her as she follows God's path."

He said things to Jay like it wouldn't be unusual to see me take part in the marches that were going on. That was when Jay hit the ceiling. He said, "Never. She needs to be home taking care of Kellie."

The conflict and the weekly calls from Mother urging me to work and educate myself while Jay demanded I get pregnant caused my health to deteriorate. By year three, I had bleeding ulcers and was hospitalized twice. My doctor, Dr. Zenbaum, said, "You must stop this damage to your intestines. You can't marry or have a day-to-day relationship with everybody you love."

When our daughter was three, Jay became insistent that I get pregnant. He wanted a son. When I told him I didn't think we were ready, he began pleading. Now in the fourth year of our marriage, in order to satisfy his wishes and my obsession to keep the marriage going, I became pregnant against the advice of my doctor. Nine months into the pregnancy, just as I began buying boy baby clothing, I was sent to the hospital to be seen immediately by a specialist.

Almost hysterical, I called my church pastor for prayer and prayed hard for my baby to live. The baby died.

Jay was wonderful, sympathetic, and caring, but I felt devastated, and the look on his face told me he was as well. Right away he suggested that we wait a few months and try again. I knew for certain I would follow doctor's orders and never ever become pregnant again. The loss of my son took a toll on my mind and body.

Although I was determined to hold my marriage together, the tension was also beginning to profoundly affect our daughter. She began stuttering and fretting, and my bleeding ulcers had not stopped. I consulted with the minister again, and he agreed that we needed some time of separation. We'd been married for six years, but I would have to leave Jay for my health and for the sake of my daughter. I sat Jay down and tried to reason with him, but he was furious. Once more I saw the minister, and he agreed with me that we would need to separate for a time.

I prayed night and day. Leaving Jay broke my heart. I had hoped we would be together forever. At that time, it was only my belief in the Lord Jesus that kept me sane. I was so lonely and frightened in the big city of San Francisco by myself with my baby that I even considered returning to Jay. I would tell him I'd do anything to be together. Ultimately, I couldn't do that because he wasn't going to change without a miracle.

Rather than any racial divide, it was our cultural differences and expectations that led to our divorce. I never felt any prejudice from Jay except against a housewife who was not longing to try new recipes, fold underwear, and fill and replace ice cube trays. We began the process of divorce, both of us sad as we declared that we loved each other.

While it is true that our daughter resembled the profile of Jay's family—green eyes, reddish-brown hair, and freckles— her appearance did not reduce my love for her. She was my baby, and I wanted custody of my baby. Jay wanted sole custody himself. I had not a dime. His parents had many resources. It appeared for a time that I would lose her. He was getting out of the army and moving home in another state. I believed if he took her, I would never see her. Once again, I began to pray as Grandmother had taught me. I kept the faith that as I was her mother, I deserved to have her live with me. Even though there seemed no way out for me, I had faith God would rescue me.

During the months that passed, I sustained myself with faith and kept busy with continued classes. I also began to recall Grandmother's notion that God has a plan for each of us. It is up to us to conform and comply. I felt more comfortable pursuing an education, knowing I would be of service.

A law professor at my university stopped me and asked why my grades were dropping and why I appeared so sad. I told him I was getting a divorce. He said, based on what he knew of me and my involvement in the Little Rock integration, he would represent me without payment, and he did. I walked out of court with an order for full custody for myself and visitation rights for Jay.

Not a day goes by that I do not think about the son I lost. Christopher is the chosen name we gave to him. Thirty years later, I was seated on the couch watching the news. The announcer presented a photo of a three-year-old boy available for adoption who resembled my daughter and what I imagined my son would have looked like. I telephoned the station to ask about the child's availability, and I was told that at age fifty I was too old to adopt him. I replied that they could not tell me that—and to send me the papers. My petition won over one hundred other inquiries.

Yes, I do often think of my ex-husband, Jay, and whether I would have preferred to have spent my life with him as a housewife. The answer is no. Had I stayed married, I would be a very different Melba.

I am the Melba God intended me to be. As Grandmother had pointed out, I used to the best of my ability the great mental capacity God had taken extra measures to ensure I had. Today, I see Jay as a gift of God, a bridge that helped repair my soul. He taught me without a doubt to trust and rid myself of any remaining vindictive thoughts. Like my white parents before him, he taught me that white is a state of mind and my freedom is up to me to choose.

I have the most positive and loving thoughts about Jay because the gift he left behind of a beautiful, charming, intelligent, and loving daughter has been mine to enjoy through all these years.

Mistakes and struggles are part of our human journey. The key is to forgive and pick ourselves up with the faith that life will improve because of lessons learned from our mistakes.

Nine

SINGLE PARENTHOOD

After the divorce, my daughter had to adjust to many changes in our lifestyle. Above all else, she missed her father because he had been a wonderful parent, playmate, and friend. She was also upset because I was forced to give up our lovely home that we had shared with her dad and move to low-income housing in the Sunnydale Housing Project. I would learn this project was an incubator for some members of the flamboyant and controversial Black Panthers.

It was 1969, a time when the Black Panthers based in Oakland, California, were growing in numbers and pressing their demands for equality. Newspapers across the United States reported on their actions. It was an environment I would later deem too dangerous for a single mother and her daughter. But back then, I didn't know any better. I was doing my best. I considered our new living arrangement as a bridge—a temporary home because we were on the waiting list for San Francisco State University student housing. Our income was severely limited while I struggled to complete a college degree that would result in a good job and elevate our lifestyle.

About six months into our stay at Sunnydale, Kellie was still going to the metal mail slot in our front door each day, pushing it open with a pencil and peeking through it, in hopes of getting a letter from her dad. She would sometimes linger there peering out at the kids playing on our sidewalk because I never allowed her to go outside.

I felt fragile and afraid of life. I realized I was in a precarious situation in every way—financially, physically, and mentally. Kellie had (at age five) grown old enough to miss her dad and to face reality while still hoping Jay would be back.

Our life in the Sunnydale Housing Project was far from the comfortable middle-class one we had shared in our home on a sunny, pristine street. Gone were the well-mannered children she could play with outside each day. We no longer had friendly, protective, religious neighbors or our cozy sense of safety and late-evening family events. Sunnydale was an experience that would teach us to deal with life on its most primitive terms. Most of the people who lived there were on welfare. As I would learn later, many were living at the edge of society, having existed in extreme poverty most of their lives.

Take, for example, the two men who came every Saturday with what appeared to be a vegetable truck. The back of the truck was lined with wooden crates filled with lovely apples, oranges, peaches, collard greens, string beans, and many other fruits and vegetables. However, when I approached the truck, it became evident it was anything but a neighborhood vegetable vendor.

The driver lifted one of the vegetable crates and beneath was every possible line of watches, silverware, telephones, and so on that you could ever want or need. His partner, one of the most elegantly dressed people I'd ever seen, said, "If you don't see what you want here, Missy, we can always get it for you. For instance, you see a dress you want at Macy's, mark down the rack, size, color, and specific location, and we'll have it for you by Wednesday, for a price of course."

"Yes, sir," I answered.

Unhinged by his offer, I grabbed Kellie's hand and pulled her close to me. He said, "We are not limited by what's here," and continued, "If you need a car, furniture, let me know what you need. The big stuff comes by ship twice a month." This tall, slender white man resembled a priest while his black partner reminded me of my Little Rock minister. Both were well spoken and well dressed.

"Thank you," I said, "I'll keep that in mind." As I rushed away, I knew I would never go near that truck again.

Because of my growing awareness that the Sunnydale project was an unsafe place for us to live, Kellie and I began to go out less and less often. We went out early in the morning to go to school and were back home by 4:00 p.m. At first, we didn't have a car and had to ride eight buses a day—two to drop Kellie off at school and two more for me to go to San Francisco State for classes and then four on the return trip. When I explained that to my mother, she said she had heard that Sunnydale was indeed dangerous and would try to get us a vehicle so we could be safer until we moved.

Both Kellie and I missed Jay. We spoke about him often, while I tried to demonstrate a calm voice for her and to build our new lives. I yearned to hear from Jay; any word would have been comforting. I found myself going through a period in which I could not take his toothbrush out of the toothbrush holder; I hung on to any small thing he had left behind. I asked myself over and over again if I had done the wrong thing by getting a divorce. Should I have been the kind of wife he wanted me to be? Should I have done whatever it took to remain in his protective cocoon, even though relinquishing a slice of myself each day I pretended? It had felt so safe—to be with him felt so good, so hopeful.

God bless television because it was Kellie's babysitter while I studied to finish my bachelor's degree. Our one big adventure each week was a trip to church, where I became a full participant and Kellie became a full-fledged member in the kiddie Sunday school. Sundays were our days off, our escape from our ghetto housing scene into the middle-class world we had come from. Once again, it took eight buses for our journey. We left at 9:00 in the morning and did not get home before 4:30 that afternoon. On the way home, we always stopped for lunch with just enough money to divide one hamburger and one orange drink. That was our once-a-week splurge.

Our budget did not allow more than that one splurge. Sometimes I had little money left over after rent and bills. In one particularly lean month, we ate spaghetti thirty days in a row. For me, it was a signal of my desperation; for Kellie, it was a period of excitement as spaghetti was her favorite food. I told her it was a big blessing because God thought we were doing well. I prayed for an answer. I was offered a job grading papers for a professor.

On one afternoon while I was deep in study upstairs and Kellie was downstairs watching television, I heard the slam of the metal cover to our mail slot. It always signaled the time when she would race to the door to look out and then collect the mail. I had pondered how I could break Kellie of the habit of pining for a letter from her dad. She would explain his actions by saying, "Daddy doesn't have a pencil" or "Daddy doesn't have a stamp." I knew for certain that wasn't the case, but if it temporarily satisfied her need, I did not tell her otherwise.

Suddenly, I was struck by a panicked thought that she should not be in that place at that time. Something was really wrong! Was I overreacting, but to what? Nothing out of the ordinary was happening, but I remembered what Grandmother had said: "God is always on your side. He is as close as your skin if you only listen." I called Kellie, "Let me read you a story." Her favorite was *Cloudy with a Chance of Meatballs*.

I called out to her again. "Kellie, if you hurry, I'll read you two stories. I'll read Dr. Seuss." I heard the sound of her footsteps on the stairs. "Meatballs, Mommy, read Meatballs and Elephant."

At that exact moment, a shot rang out, hitting the letter slot. I grabbed Kellie, pulled her near me, and ducked under the bed. I heard more shots, then police cars and loud voices right outside. The bullet had splintered our door. I shuddered to think what would have happened had Kellie been standing there as usual. "Thank You, God, for letting my baby live," I whispered. Now I knew we had to get out of there. The police told me it was the result of Panther gang activities. "You must have someone watching over you, someone powerful."

"God is the most powerful," I responded.

I had to do whatever it took to get away. I prayed hard and went every day to the student housing office to check on my application. Within three weeks of my doubled prayers, we moved to the San Francisco State student housing village. We would be in walking distance of the university and surrounded by other college students and their families. Every night during the first several months there, we both got on our knees and gave thanks to God for our safe and cozy new home.

There in that village I met many people who were kind to us. Some of them would take care of us and teach us the ropes of living in the village. Others would give us rides. Soon, with help from my mother and a partial student loan, I was able to get a car, a Volkswagen Bug.

This period in student housing was the beginning of a light at the end of our tunnel. Kellie attended the elementary school on campus, cutting out our long commute; we had more time at home together. She was able to play at playgrounds and have friends in this international community.

I met many teachers who would become mentors. One in particular, Lynn Ludlow, began to guide me in my desire to become a journalist. He convinced me that, although my spelling was off, I was an excellent news writer. "The great James Joyce could not spell, like many of our authors."

I joined the San Francisco State journalism newspaper and was awarded several prizes for my reporting and writing. During the last year of our stay at the university, we were beginning to heal our wounds from the divorce. Kellie stopped looking for mail from her dad, and I removed his toothbrush from the holder. We both soaked ourselves in a new life, growing ever busier. I sought and received an internship from the local CBS television newsroom. Kellie took African dance lessons and began playing the piano.

Not long before graduation, Professor Ludlow asked me if I knew anything about the Columbia University New York program in broadcast journalism. I did not. He said it was a program in which thirty-five minority students from across the United States would be trained in television news and granted full-time jobs in the industry when they finished. Those chosen would get a scholarship worth more than $50,000, free room and board, a graduate degree, and an opportunity to appear on national TV. I submitted my application on a Friday afternoon and didn't think much more about it. Three days later, I was asked to fly to New York to try out.

Indeed, by the grace of God, I was chosen. With my selection came a guaranteed job on public television as a journalist. This scholarship was a kick start for my career. I was placed in a position that would have taken me perhaps years and years to achieve. Instead of struggling to attain a job in a market (San Francisco) that ranked seventh in the nation, I would go to New York right after university.

The following May, I graduated. We didn't have the funds for Mother Lois to come from Little Rock; Kellie and I sat alone. As they called the names of the graduates, their families and friends applauded for them. When my name was called, there was total silence. A six-feet-six Rastafarian friend of mine stood up and shouted, "You better give Mamma your hand because she done come all this way from Little Rock, Arkansas, to earn this degree. It's been a long road. Give it up for her."

The audience stood on its feet and applauded. I marched forward with tears in my eyes as little Kellie ran up to greet me.

The path on life's journey of single parenthood is eased by trusting in God and knowing that our child is also a child of God and He loves us both. He is with us and providing for our needs even before we know what they are.

Ten

DON'T LET ANYONE STEAL YOUR DREAMS

My encounters with news reporters during my Little Rock experience had sparked a desire in me to become a news reporter. The reporters in some way became the voice for us who had not been heard before. I marveled at how they took command of any event they approached and how much in charge they were as they worked to present both sides of the story in an unbiased way. I noticed how speedy and self-confident they were. They were also the first people to make me feel as though I had an opinion that counted. I had always read the news, and now I faithfully listened to the news on the radio and watched it on television.

Most of the reporters and cameramen were white. A very few were African American, but they too had that air of assurance that they were in charge. I was drawn to their self-confidence and their conviction that what they were doing was right and honorable.

I wondered then if I could become a news reporter. It frightened me when the African American reporters and cameramen were terribly beaten up by the mob gathered in front of Central High who was set on keeping us out even if they had to kill us.

During my four years as an undergraduate, I had been an editor for the student newspaper. This job included collecting news stories and directing those on my team to collect and write the news as well. This job was second nature to me because I loved it so much and got along with the almost all-white student body without any drama.

Upon acceptance to the program at Columbia University, I arranged for my mother to take care of Kellie in Little Rock. Then in anticipation of leaving San Francisco and heading to New York for the program, I got a physical exam by my physician, Dr. Zenbaum, whom I highly respected and adored. He had always been very cordial and respectful of me in every way. He had nourished me through childbirth, my divorce, and several bouts of pneumonia and had always encouraged me to attend school.

Throughout my troubled marriage and now as a single parent struggling to regain my stability, I found he and his wife to be kind, generous, and encouraging. Certainly, he had proven himself to be someone who was supportive and caring. That was why I decided to tell him my good news.

"I'm so happy," I said to him. "I've been granted a scholarship to attend a journalism program at Columbia University."

"What do you mean?" he asked.

"I'm going to be a news reporter. I want to work for a local station," I said.

"You can't become a television news reporter—not in this day and age. You are, after all, African American and too fat!"

I couldn't believe these words from the man to whom I dared reveal my secret hope, the man I'd hoped would give me words of encouragement.

He continued, "Unrealistic dreams are a sign of mental problems. It will make you very unhappy to want something you can never have."

Holding on to my dignity, not wanting to display my wounded response to his pronouncement, I waited until I got out of his office to cry. What he said was very disarming. I thought, *Was he right? Was there a position for a person who looked like me? Could I really do this incredible job?*

When a person of his caliber questions your ability, it scatters your dreams into a thousand pieces, and you have to re-collect them, assemble them, and hold on to the images all over again. "God, please," I whispered, "please guide me to where You want me to be. You said no human voice could dictate my future. It will be up to You."

A few days later, I boarded the plane to Little Rock and took my daughter to remain with my mother while I pursued my degree. I was so grateful Mother had agreed to keep her.

Two years passed. I had returned to California to start my position as a news reporter at KQED, the local PBS station, on their 7:00 p.m. nightly *Newsroom* program. When I took my place on that historic set, the people I admired were sitting on either side of me. I couldn't believe it.

All the pieces of my dream had come together. Indeed, I had climbed another mountain, and it would become the main route over the bridge to equality and a primer to understanding the world. Observing and reporting and covering state, county, city, national, and international news, I learned things I could not have learned in books. I learned again to trust my dreams to no one except God on high.

A year later, I was employed in the seventh largest television market in the nation at NBC in San Francisco. One of the secretaries informed me that Dr. Zenbaum had called to invite me to dinner at his house. I declined, as I was sure he had done so only to show his friends that he knew me. By that time, I had found another physician.

Do not count on other humans to have faith in your dreams. It is your commitment and faith in God that turns dreams into reality.

Eleven

GOD GRANTS DREAMS BIGGER THAN YOU IMAGINE

On my first day of work, I stood outside KQED, San Francisco's public broadcasting station. I felt as though I were falling off a mountainside. After all, the people I was about to work with were the people I had watched on my television each weekday evening in the show called *Newsroom*. These were respected news professionals—I was Miss Nobody. I took a deep breath and stepped over the edge, trusting that God would protect and guide me.

The faces I had seen on my TV screen came alive as I took my place at the *Newsroom* desk for my first broadcast. My heart was pounding in my chest, beating loud and fast in my ears. On that first night, seated at the round table amid the expert reporters I so respected, I mispronounced the word *Massachusetts*. I wanted to fly away, but I survived to make it through the day and to settle into my news reporting job.

As time passed, I began to feel like I too could become good at reporting.

My time at KQED was a grand experience. The pros took me under their wings and nurtured me, sharing the skills they had acquired. Known for its liberal philosophy and diversity, this mature group enfolded me and made me feel secure. I learned so much about news gathering and reporting and life itself that I barely had enough space in my head to file my new knowledge. Above all else, they made me feel that I was their equal and my work was important.

I prayed, "Thank You, God; I have arrived. I have reached a place in my life where financially my daughter and I are secure." I was able to find an apartment in a great location where the landlord treated me not as a black person out of place but as a human being. I had a nice, late-model car to drive. *This must be how the world really works in California,* I thought to myself. *All the hard work I did was worthwhile.*

I was feeling very confident. I took a deep breath. I was forging my way through competition and struggling to learn new information. I felt as if I was now far beyond the racism of Little Rock, far beyond the vivid oppression I had endured during my youth. Perhaps some of these California people understood the meaning of equality.

Less than a year later, I was offered a job at KRON TV, NBC's local affiliate. Stunned at the enormity of this job, I was once again in awe of all of my broadcast partners and full of gratitude for the incredible opportunity. Faith sustained me as my life whirled about as though I were in a giant mixer. Suddenly, people recognized me and asked for my autograph—I got special tables in restaurants without asking. I had to stop going to the grocery store midday and shop at 9:00 p.m. to avoid clamoring shoppers who followed me around.

The bling and money offered me by the station were beyond comprehension. I began to feel comfortable and much more important. I found a church where Kellie and I followed the process Grandmother and Mother had engrained in me. I struggled for grounding and connection with God. I learned to deal with the headlines that tear you apart. I had become one of the first female reporters in San Francisco and the first African American granted the post of an on-air news reporter with a major network.

I had not anticipated what it would mean to grace the world from behind a television camera. People I did not know spoke to me and expected me to speak back. I began to get requests for public appearances as I once had ten years before as one of the Little Rock Nine.

I was the only African American female in my newsroom, and after a few months I noticed that, from time to time, the other reporters had a subtle way of making me feel less than. No one called me nigger; no white-sheeted people rode past me carrying crosses. Instead, I was not invited to newsroom parties in people's homes, not included in newsroom social life. Invitations were whispered around the room. Discussions of celebrations held the night before leaked out and spilled over me.

I was not often assigned stories that assured high placement in the newscast. I attributed that to both my gender and my race. I was relegated to lightweight stories assigned to what people in the industry called "the monkey on display in the window." Each television station had one African American as evidence of their dutiful willingness to fulfill demands for equality in the news industry, and they displayed them as often as possible. Even when I found a more important story and investigated it on my own—a story that should have been labeled significant news—it was given to someone else to cover on air. I was relegated to doing the legwork—investigating.

It took more than a year for me to recognize and define the new job oppression I faced. It had become easy for me to respond to obvious Little Rock segregation. But I didn't know how to respond to the subtle, but no less vicious, oppression that pierced heart, soul, and mind as much as ropes and guns.

The realization crept up on me that I was facing an institutional and entrenched form of bullying. The question was, how was I to respond? I spoke with a black female who was ten years older than I and had been a real pioneer in the industry. She confirmed what I suspected and said it resembled the path I had taken in Central High, only subtler and slightly less hazardous. "You are fighting for equality, but here oppression sneaks up on you, and before you know it, you are on your knees if you don't protect yourself," she said. "It is much more difficult when you are isolated and alone."

No one shot me down physically; they merely shot my spirit down. They attacked my spirit in ways I didn't notice at first, nor did I realize that I wasn't getting all I deserved. What was unclear to me was how to defend myself with dignity.

Bullies made it clear their prejudice was not just because of my color but because of my gender as well. The fact is there were few females in newsrooms in the late 1970s. If they were in the newsroom, they were usually carrying coffee and serving some support function and were not professional news gatherers. As time passed, I was taunted by stress and fear and apprehension. Who would attack next—when and where? When would a seemingly clever line other folks laughed aloud at be the knife in my back?

One day, I stepped into the newsroom early in the morning wearing curlers and on my way to makeup. I was preparing to sit at the news desk at the noon broadcast to introduce an important story I had covered. It had taken two years to get to this place, and I was proud because it was a step up the ladder. It was the first day I would be going "live" on air on the news desk.

As I ventured farther into the room on this Tuesday morning, there was a group of videographers, reporters, and staff standing nearby. I peered down at the green shoulder bag that held my suit for the day. It felt as though it was slipping off my shoulder so I paused to collect myself.

"Aunt Jemima, ain't you got no pancake mix to fix my breakfast?" one of the cameramen I'll call Ray suddenly called out. I stood frozen in my tracks with my heart bleeding pain. What an awful insult! The name "Aunt Jemima" has long been offensive to black women, indicating black women could only be cooks.

Time flashed backward for a moment. It was an insult referencing slavery. Was this the side door of Central High? Who were these people who said things like that? I didn't know what to do. Tears stung my eyes. How did other people of color respond to this? What did he expect me to do? Why did he say it? Why did he call me a name and refer to this insulting image? Had I done something to bring on this outcry? Was this the beginning, and was I going to become the in-house target? I was compelled to push back immediately.

For some twenty-five times over the past year, I had ignored their insults and turned the other cheek in silence, but that was not working. I thought for a moment about the phrase someone had pasted on top of my computer: "Sweet Melba." Up to that time, I had been labeled as cooperative, a good reporter, and most of all, conciliatory. I had never begun a row over issues that involved the question of race, nor had I responded to those who spewed insults prior to today.

Had I relinquished my role as a civil rights warrior? Quickly I whispered, "Help me, God." And then I knew it was time to speak up. This man's total disrespect of me in front of many of my other colleagues had drawn a line in the sand, and I stepped over it. I had to make him pull his foot back. The question was, how? After pondering for a long moment, I fired my cannon back at him as hard as I could with firm dignity. Silence froze the room. His eyes grew huge, and his face grew red. He looked at me with an astonished expression. I turned and walked away.

I remembered the words of Martin Luther King Jr., who said, no matter what, we should maintain our dignity. At that point, I knew I would no longer give up my dream of equality in exchange for oppression and blatant assault in order to become a news reporter. I was passionate about being a respected and equal news gatherer and news reporter. It was not only what I pleaded for but also what I demanded. I reported Ray's behavior to the supervisor and said, "If you cannot correct this, I will have to go to the NAACP and the press with it. I know for certain that sponsors do not want this kind of publicity.

"We can't be included in the process if our point of view is not heard," I said. "We must have a voice, just as you have a voice." The Civil Rights organization labored long and hard for access to objective and fair inclusion in the news process.

From that moment forward, people treated me with a different attitude. They no longer brought over pictures of stars eating watermelon and asked me what clubs they belonged to, no longer made any joke that was inappropriate. They knew that although I had not responded to their pranks in the past, I was prepared to do so from now on. I would not be a punching bag or a deposit for their insensitive or off-color jokes.

Had I mistaken the comfort of a good salary, a super job, and public fame for God's mission? Had I really taken my church membership seriously and kept my commitment to the Lord Jesus, or was I substituting worldly comfort? I began asking myself many questions.

As time passed, I began to feel that maybe my heavenly assignment was to break down walls of segregation with dignity. I continued to find myself as the first person of color in various positions, meeting face-to-face with bully racists determined to derail me. Over and over again, as I sought careers as a public relations specialist, a professor, and a businesswoman, the same issues arose. Over and over again, my grandmother's words came to me: "Why go where you're not welcome? Because if you go only where others welcome you, you are confined to surrender to the choices of others. Claim what you want to belong to first."

I now realized that segregation, separateness, and oppression were not things I was going to erase immediately, no matter the location. Changes would come about in God's time. However, with that understanding came a reflection of my experience of racial prejudice in its interwoven, complex layers in socializing, assignments, amenities, promotions, real friendships, and recognition for a job well done. These instances had to be assessed carefully. I did not want to become paranoid nor be accused of "playing the color card," a victim whom white folks labeled a constant complainer.

At first, it was disappointing and heartbreaking to realize that each and every wall of prejudice would take time to come down. There were no instant solutions. I thought to myself that my assignment from God seemed to be a lifelong project. Indeed, protection and equality could not always be found even in California, at least not in my experience.

Nevertheless, with faith and prayer, I braced myself and proceeded to carve a path that would hopefully leave a trail for others of color to follow—Central High had been a good lesson. I had to count my blessings and recognize the progress made. As Grandma advised, I had to keep my eyes on the prize—to define my purpose and my assignment from God!

Faith must be sustained, especially through disillusionment and delayed outcomes hoped and prayed for: "In God's time, only in God's time."

Twelve

TURNING THE OTHER CHEEK

As a Christian who is often taunted and excluded by folks who set up categories of "other" for the people who are different, I have had to learn specific skills to know how and when to respond so that I can live in peace as Jesus would have me live. Whether the labeling is based on appearance, language, culture, religion, age, or gender, it takes a special set of skills to respond only when absolutely necessary. For me, exclusion is most often because of the color of my skin. That means for those who see "other" as a category, I am always labeled because my difference is so apparent.

I believe that among those skills one must learn, the first is the art of turning the other cheek. This process, which is explained in the Bible, is essential to healthy survival. I am unable to always be a warrior in the ready-to-attack mode. That would take much time away from prayer and study.

The second skill is the practice of gracefully sinking into golden silence when need be and identifying when it is time to speak up. Grandma said, "Jesus was never a wimp. He faced enemies and negative situations when need be—always obeying the instruction in the Bible to do unto others as you would have them do unto you."

There is no need to loudly announce one's strategy as a way of threatening one's opponent. The best solution of all is to smile and walk away in silence, wishing your would-be attacker the best of everything, thus employing the third skill—which is patience.

When properly used, all these skills are seated in the basic trust that God is stronger than any enemy and will resolve the issue in time. Having faith in God let me consistently work at developing these skills so that I could grow an antenna to guide me in discerning whether using my energy to defend myself is tantamount to my survival or a waste of my time and energy. I must always ask myself, "Is fighting back in this particular instance, even in the face of inappropriate words or violent action, in compliance with God's request to do unto others as you would have done to you?" Of course, it is important that I follow God's words to treat others as equals; seeing equal is an essential quest for being seen as equal.

Today, the most intense periods in which I get to use these skills of turning the other cheek and patience are when I go house hunting. My patience is often worn thin, and I become anxious to conclude the tedious process in order to settle into what is to become my next home.

I have concluded that house hunting is still an area of challenge despite the progress we've made in human rights. It remains a horrible reminder of bias for many people of color, the elderly, the LGBT community, or the disabled, who are all victims of labeling for one reason or another. House hunting is a heartbreaking chore. It leaves me feeling powerless and less valued or unequal because my home is the center of my stability.

Living in California in 2017, I like to feel all should be well and that I am just another Christian American, "free at last" from the confines of the South. Having recently moved, I was jarred into realizing that all is not well—in fact, I am still "other." I must continue to trust Jesus as my home because of his biblical promise: "In my Father's house are many rooms. If it were not so, would I have told *you* that *I go* to *prepare a place* for *you*?" (John 14:2 ESV, emphasis added).

Just now, after some sixty years of living in California on the opposite side of the country from the oppression I grew up in, I find I must still be patient. There has not been a lot of progress in the granting of rights about who will accept whom as a next-door neighbor.

Any decision to take up house hunting includes a decision to be patient and to turn the other cheek. My rule for myself is that if the potential landlord shows me any unwelcome signs, I turn and rush for the car. My conclusion is that house hunting does not leave me the energy to change people's minds and help them face their evolution into civility. I am not there to instigate civil rights upgrades or to create integration in housing. That is a task for another time and another place.

I've run into Christian Americans labeled "other" who said they have felt the sting of exclusion when the owner or renter merely suspected they were black. Take the experience of my white colleague who said she was attempting to rent in Philadelphia. When she phoned for an apartment, the owners turned her down because, as they later said, they believed she was black. When her white-sounding husband phoned about the same apartment, they welcomed him to come and see it and were happy to offer him a rental contract.

As I begin this task, I know that I am going to collect enough mysterious experiences to rattle my nerves. Let's start with a memory that demonstrates exclusion can be fun. About twenty years ago when my network news cameraman Billy and I were covering a story, we drove slowly down the street of an upscale San Francisco neighborhood looking for the location of the story. We parked in front of a beautiful house and looked at our notes to determine the specific address. At first, we did not notice the For Sale sign.

The moment we parked, however, the man across the street, who was running his lawn mower, cut the engine and rushed across to talk to us. His flushed red face and lined expression let me know he was anxious and angry. His words confirmed my suspicion. He began, "Are you house hunting? Don't stop here. . . . You're not trying to buy this house, are you? It's not really available, you know. You should keep looking, but not in this area."

"What do you mean, not available to me?" Billy said with anger crowning his voice.

"Well, you won't be happy here. It's not for you. There are none of your people living around here."

We smiled, and that's when Billy nudged me in the side to indicate we could have a little fun.

"Yeah, tell us about the neighborhood. We're here to get a house," Billy said.

We looked at each other and said, "Let's go for it," as the man's face turned absolutely bright red. We quickly got out of the car and headed for the front lawn.

Billy said, "Do you think we can put the barbeque right here on the front lawn, darling?"

The red-faced man replied, "Oh my God, are you kidding?" He suddenly donned the role of the hostile plantation owner. "Oh no, we don't barbeque on the front lawn. Who would barbeque in the front yard? I tell you. You really can't afford this place."

"Oh yeah, haven't you seen her on the news?" Billy turned me around to face the man.

"They're determined to get top dollar, you know. There's a lot wrong with the house."

I took a tape measure and began stretching it from the edge of the porch to where the barbeque would go. We continued our conversation with comments like, "We could put the lawn chairs there on the left. The green ones, honey."

"Yup, the green ones," Billy said.

The more intense we got with our fictitious decorating plan, the angrier our hostile advisor became and the more reasons he came up with as to why we couldn't have the house. We let him rev himself into a lather before we finally told him we could afford the house, but we were not interested in it. We were actually looking for Mrs. Covington because we were reporters looking for her story.

That's when he started to clasp his hands, bow, back away with a smile, and feign an apology. "Of course, I'd never want to keep you out," he said.

"Of course not." We bid him adieu. I couldn't help remembering all the times I had been house hunting and run into scenes like that with homeowners trying to fend me off.

Many dramatic scenes return in memory each time I go out to chase a new home, along with a bundle of apprehension in my stomach. Several times, the realtor would take my paperwork with the statement that I ranked high among the applicants and with a certainty I would get the place. A few hours later, she would call back and let me know I didn't get it but didn't say why.

Several instances stand out in my mind, particularly because the agent or owner hurt my heart and made me angry and frightened because they made me feel powerless. There was never anything I could do, short of hiring an attorney and suing. That takes a modicum of energy and mental focus—it drowns one.

Just last year, my daughter and I looked at nearly a hundred houses. I also had friends and coworkers looking on my behalf. I would be remiss not to mention that with the internet and social media, house hunting for "others" has improved over the years.

One of my finds was a beautiful house on the edge of the bay, which I approached on the arm of my son. "Oh, you must have the wrong address," the older, gray-haired man said in a tone so insolent I couldn't get past it. "We don't rent to your kind here. You know, it's just not for seniors. Living with the chill of the water exacerbates arthritis." When I plowed my way through his physical excuses, he went to "Well, you know, there really are none of your people out here. You'd probably get lonely!"

In that moment, I thought lawsuits, shotguns, someone to beat him up—and then the lines that have sustained me

throughout my adulthood came to me: "I go before you . . ."
I don't want to be where I am unwanted. I don't want to
fight for the privilege to be in my own home. I know that a
really nasty landlord can make a torture chamber of your
home because I have experienced it. Indeed, there have been
times when I have been told a place was not available and
called back in another voice, only to be told, "It's available.
Come right over."

For that one moment, once again, I considered a lawsuit for
the benefit of others, but it takes time and energy that I didn't
have. What fascinated me most was how gut-wrenching the
dramatics could be and the very different ways used by unwelcoming people to disenfranchise you, to convince you that
you don't really want it: you don't know your own feelings,
it's not appropriate for you, it's unsafe for you to be there,
this is not your kind of neighborhood, there's a bear in the
bushes. They would go to any lengths to convince you that
you don't want the place.

They were unimaginable scenarios. One summer afternoon, as a single empty nester at about age fifty, I went house
hunting in beautiful, hillside Sausalito, California, where I
always wanted to live. Everyone said it was the place God
sent people when there was no room in heaven. This coastal
village is cozy, elegant, and beautiful—a tourist favorite and
where families feel safe to rear children.

I knocked on six doors listed; each time, I was told that if
only I had arrived a few minutes earlier I could have had the
place, but it had just been rented. "I'd better take the sign
down," the landlord would say.

If I drove away and then returned a little while later, the
sign would be back up. In one case, I knocked on the door

again and asked if the possible renter had let the place go and if it was available as the sign was back up. I was told, "Oh, is that sign back up? It must have walked out there on its own. I'd better get it back again."

"May God bless" were words I walked away saying.

Living in a world in which we stand out for one reason or another requires us to be even closer to God and have the faith to know that we are not required to fight every battle.

Thirteen

GOD IS MY EMPLOYER

By 1975, the feeling of stability I had experienced at the Mc-Cabes and the brief feeling of comfort I had felt as Jay's wife and the triumph I had enjoyed on my television job began to disappear within a dust cloud of Little Rock panic. Again, it was clear I had to function in warrior mode. I could not lay down my Little Rock, Arkansas, suit of armor. This was just a different battle.

My heart ached. Each day that passed, I could see more of what was going on around me. I allowed myself to face reality. I experienced opportunities each day to ignore hints of racism and sexism on my job. I had to admit that California was not the promised land. Rather, God had presented a new type of challenge. I assumed this must be a test of some kind that I could not afford to fail for my sake and the sake of those who came behind me!

As a news reporter, I played a double role in the pool of "other": the first as an African American and the second as a woman. In the beginning, I smiled and watched as the assignment editor presented the real, hard news stories to the men while I and the one other staff female were both assigned the fluffy stories, such as the crocheting festival for a charity fund-raiser, allowable fashions for the university, or household products detrimental to the body. When the news came on at 5:00, the stories we were assigned ran either at the end of the program or not at all because they had been dumped. I was quite restless, wondering if I would ever get a story with teeth in it. Then one day, an urgent call came on the radio while I was in the field covering a nonsense story. I was directed to turn around and go to a nearby location.

The assignment editor said, "You are the nearest, and we will send a male to follow up because this appears to be a grisly story." I made my way to the scene praying out loud that this would be a chance to prove my reporting skills. The cameraman responded, "This, in the year of our Lord 1975, when women are supposed to be equal, especially in this business."

As I drew near to the car, I could see there was blood dripping out of the trunk and blood smeared all over the car. Almost immediately, three male reporters from a competing station gathered around me and began treating me as though I was the little woman.

"Let us handle this for you, Melba. Just step back and we'll do the work for you."

"Do you want to go back to the car? We'll come over with all the details."

"Get her some water."

Five uniformed policemen approached with lots of equipment, cameras, and plastic bags with which to gather evidence. The tall, red-haired one spoke to me.

"Listen, little lady, what are you doing? Who do you represent?" I showed him my credentials. "We'll get you a chair, and you sit over here, as we think there are bodies in that car."

It was then that I gathered all my spiritual strength and determined I had to behave with dignity for myself and all the other women in the field. I didn't want to do anything that would justify unequal assignments. I lowered my head and said the Lord's Prayer and prayed, "Please, God, give me the strength to show them who I am."

The policeman shrugged and went to the scene. As his colleagues took fingerprints off the back of the car, I became overcome by the stench of the bodies and the sight of the blood and was only seconds away from passing out on the ground. Suddenly, the policeman who had been taking fingerprints turned the key in the trunk lock and started lifting it up. I was no more than three feet away and felt my head reeling. I prayed, "God, I am Your child, and I know that You are here with me no matter what my mind sees."

Then I stiffened my knees and looked at the rim of the trunk, knowing that those bodies were God's children too, and He would take care of them as well. At that moment, the camera light started to flash and the cameras started to spin. The moment the trunk opened, the male reporters all gasped. The man to the right of me put his arm around my shoulders and pulled me closer. I stiffened my body and thanked him and continued to keep the look of a professional reporter. When we had our information, we all turned and moved over to get details from the policeman in charge.

I felt gratitude in my heart because, with the help of Christ Jesus, I had made it. The men around me began to compliment me for being that strong. They hadn't thought a woman would be able to do it. They said they knew I was new on-board and now realized I was going to be real competition. I had proven myself and climbed out of the "other" category. It would take another two years before I would win awards and become known as an excellent hard-news reporter, proficient at everything from murder trials to on-site crimes.

Soon, some of the other women (there were three working in San Francisco at the time) thanked me for what I had done because it elevated their status as reporters. We women reporters sometimes met over weekend lunch to discuss how much we disliked the fluffy assignments and what measures we might take. Indeed, patience was our tool, while we worked hard to practice and improve our reporting skills. I became known as a cowgirl because I could ride with the cowboys, covering such stories as Chinatown gangs, Patty Hearst, and the Zebra murders.

From then on, my concern about battling racism and sexism was added to the daily dynamic and stressful grind of reporting the news. It was a fast-paced mix of emotion in response to human suffering and sometimes hopeless situations. For example, there was the morning I was called to a scene where an eight-year-old had been crushed beneath the wheels of a streetcar, and his mother stood by waiting for him to be removed. She was inconsolable, and I felt I should help her in some way. Nevertheless, I had to move on to cover a Berkeley University student march.

I was conflicted. "Is this routine of rushing through tragic events making me callous?" I asked myself. At first, I was angry, asking God, "Why me?" I had to pray my way into peace, hoping I could redefine my role. What was I here for? What must I do? What did God expect of me? Where did I belong as an African American? And would I ever be able to live without racism, or would I always have to struggle to experience a modicum of equality?

Being a news reporter and a single parent also often caused conflict in the use of my time. Working as a reporter requires one to be available at all hours of the day or night. Take, for example, the Patty Hearst/SLA kidnap incident on February 4, 1974. *NBC News* called me out of bed at midnight to cover the story. I had to drop off my daughter, wrapped up in a blanket, at the next-door neighbor's house. I was on duty covering that story for the next twenty-four hours.

Over the years, as I proved my strength and determination, I was assigned to follow many hard-core crime cases and, indeed, became one of the station's female experts. I refused to be assigned to grocery store prices and embroidery stories, like some assignments editors still doled out to women. I complained and dug hard for the real stories. I returned to school to study law one night a week.

Finally, I was covering the story of San Francisco's famous "Zebras," a group of Black Muslims who rampaged through the city, shooting citizens at random. The entire city of San Francisco panicked during the horrifying months that people were killed for no reason. I could not forget details of each victim's death. In addition to following the police hunt for the criminals, I covered the trial for more than a year. By the end, I had exacerbated my nerves, sitting in court six hours a day. I was exhausted of crime.

Being a news cowgirl meant a hectic schedule that was uncomfortable for me and my twelve-year-old daughter. One day, I was introducing a story live on the air when, to my surprise, the camera stopped filming at a time other than when the script read "Commercial Break." The director walked to my desk with a fearful expression and said, "Beals, you better take this crazy phone call. It sounds urgent. I will cover you for sixty seconds with a commercial."

My heart pounded. He would never make such a move except in an emergency situation.

"I got your daughter," the voice growled on the other end. "That will be one million dollars if you ever want to see her again!"

Fighting back tears, I looked at the producer. The director started the countdown to resume the broadcast. As a professional, I had no choice but to blink back my tears and complete the newscast. I quickly telephoned a male friend and asked that he find Kellie and bring her to me. I completed the broadcast, and the phone call came that my friend had found my daughter. I left work, packed her bag, and sent her off to the Russian River to stay with friends until I could assure her safety with me.

I began facing the prospect of giving up a great paycheck and looking for something different, something calm and safe for my Kellie and me. The joy of the newscaster job was that it was like a primer, an encyclopedia of life, and every day I learned something new. It revealed so much about other cultures and what it meant to be wealthy, powerful, and content. I became an observer, taking in the information as fast as I could and yearning to know more about places I'd never been and things I'd never done. There was a huge part of me that regretted giving it all up. The other part of me knew that if I didn't leave, I wouldn't be Melba. I would lose myself and Kellie in pursuit of that job. Therefore, I submitted my resignation to my boss, who urged me to rethink my decision.

Suddenly, I found myself without a job. My mother repeated to me by phone what Grandmother had always said: "You do not work for individuals; you work for God. Pray hard and figure out what your Creator wants you to do now."

Six months passed. I was spending my savings at a nerve-racking rate, even though I was enjoying my time of mothering my daughter and taking a deep breath. A friend invited me to attend one of the city's socialite roundtable lunches at which controversial topics were discussed. It was an intellectual think tank.

Seated beside me at a table for twenty dignitaries was the San Francisco bureau chief of *People* magazine. She asked if I would like to write a story for *People*. That was the beginning of a career in magazine writing.

For a time, writing for magazines was successful. More than anything, it gave me time to be a mom to Kellie and provided the kind of income that sustained us in our home. Here again, I found myself in territory uncharted by African American reporters. I was assigned to write several stories on rock-and-roll groups—that is, Journey, the Grateful Dead, the Eagles, and Eddie Money. This period in my life was lots of fun but also full of peril. Stars could not believe their eyes when I identified myself as the magazine reporter critiquing their music.

Because most of these groups had not been exposed to black writers during the '70s and '80s, I often had to jump through hoops and overlook insults in order to get them to take me seriously. I told myself I could open doors for those who followed. I prayed for God to help me, and each time I was successful. Not only did I get a story and get paid for the job, but I also built a reputation that would support other people of color who would come after me. I always left behind one message: "Yes, some African Americans do play your music. I do. So beware of your words and performances."

Like my news reporting career, magazine writing taught me much about society, business, entertainment, and economic how-tos, which led me to my idea of opening a public relations business.

Public relations is the flip side of news reporting. I used my writing skills to provide information meant to garner publicity for clients, such as nonprofits seeking to raise money or new businesses looking for customers. Writing for magazines and the public relations business required a lot of adjustment. I had to develop faith that even though I could not always see a job and security in the immediate future, they were there. There was always a next client, another magazine needing a new story. Patience and discipline were the keys to survival.

Meanwhile, Kellie was growing up fast and enjoying having a mom who could spend more time with her and still earn a living. I realized she would soon be leaving for college and on her own. I was grateful to have this time with her. I was especially anxious when she skipped a school grade and was two years younger than most in her classroom.

However, I began experiencing feelings of insecurity each day, as though I were suspended at the edge of a cliff, peering over. I was afraid I could not help myself nor count on God to do so. I clung to my church, read my Bible, and began a series of spiritual study classes.

I found I had to be steadfastly loyal to my Bible and my church. With the uncertainty of my work life, I needed to feel close to God every moment of the day. I was in a place I had never imagined, but it felt as though I was in a place I ought to be.

I began a process of building a set of habits that shut out distractions like phone calls from housewife friends who assumed, because it was the middle of the day, I could chit-chat. I was compelled to set up rigid routines in my life—priorities that yielded clients and opportunities for writing. I had to build faith in God as my employer. I remained self-employed—an employee of God—for more than twenty years with the help of discipline and guided by faith in God and myself.

I started to explore the idea of writing books at this time. This still took extraordinary discipline and trust that my writing was good enough to, in some way, serve God's purpose and, at the same time, carry a message of interest to many people.

I began a book about my early life. What a struggle, page after page, attempting to recall and record my feelings about growing up black in the South in the '40s, '50s, and '60s and my survival of the Central High firestorm and the transition to California. I could not know in the beginning that my faith and discipline over several years of life would result in *Warriors Don't Cry*, a book that has sold more than a million copies and still sells today. Faith and trust practiced with patience worked for me in what I pray is a book that continues to serve God's purpose.

———

God is our employer, no matter who we see as our earthly boss. At all times we must be aware that we are serving God in our work. It is up to us to build trust and discipline to complete God's tasks.

Fourteen

SERVING OTHERS AND SERVING GOD

For many years, I had assumed my relationship with God was one-sided. If I prayed and controlled my behavior as best I could, God would answer my prayers, maybe not in the specific way I requested, but in the way He deemed best.

However, as time passed I began to see that every day in every way God expected things of me. As I thought back, Grandmother had talked about it, and the Bible spoke of it. Now I gave more thought to what it meant to selfishly satisfy my own needs. What did God expect?

One day, I was moving and desperately needed help. I had prayed about assistance with packing as I could not pay much. A friend told me she would have her son come to help. She would pay him because he could use some time with me. "You're so spiritual," she said, "so goody-two-shoes, so righteous. Maybe it will rub off." He had been a troublesome teenager who worked hard at embarrassing her as she struggled to be a good single parent.

Her son was a handsome sixteen-year-old who took instruction well. My friend had said he needed time with me because I had proven myself full of faith, but I wondered why. He began packing boxes with vigor and speed as we worked beside each other. I offered him snacks and a sandwich, and all was going well.

Then he began to ask questions. "Do you believe in God? Do you believe there is some man out there in the clouds taking care of us?"

"Absolutely," I said, "not necessarily in the clouds, but there is always someone at our back, on our side. I wouldn't be alive without God!"

"Oh, you're one of those people like my mama. You believe there's some big angel on high making everything right. I don't agree."

"Oh yes," I said, "there's somebody there. There is also a part of that God right here inside you and me."

On and on he went through the afternoon with deep-seated questions about God. I realized as we talked that he was definitely at a turning point in his life, wondering what he should or shouldn't do.

He hinted he had friends who were not living a Christian life. He even spoke of selling drugs as being so much more lucrative than working at McDonald's.

"Yes, but if you work at McDonald's, you can smile into your own face in the mirror and sleep soundly at night, right?"

As we talked about right and wrong, selling guns, taking drugs, or being out of control, I realized he was opening his heart to me, asking things that really bothered him but things he couldn't query his mother about.

I also realized at that moment that God had decided while I needed this young man to pack and carry my boxes, perhaps he needed me more to transect the load of crucial decisions he faced. When he left, he thanked me for being nonjudgmental and sincere and for sharing my feelings with him. I had made him think and, hopefully, in a positive way.

With every part of me, I knew I was meant to have him over at that moment because he needed me as much as I needed him. That was a God assignment to fulfill my obligation for my reciprocal agreement with God. I realized then that God always had moments when He called on me to do things for others as part of His plan. Up until this time, I had not recognized this aspect of my relationship with God.

Prior to that day, I'd looked at my relationship with God like one with a genie. I asked God for His help assuming nothing would be required of me. That notion is far from the truth, and yet it is often where our egos take us. I want to believe that I am in charge and can summon the genie God to do my work with no expectation of return on my part. The more I explored the topic, the more I was shown it was a lie.

I believe I am put into close proximity with certain people for a reason. It is not an accident. It is usually based on some God assignment to help each other to see the light on our paths.

One example is when I had asked God to sustain me in my effort to become more disciplined in my writing and work to build a PR business. I promised God I would cut out my habit of watching soap operas and spend that time building my business so as to be able to serve my daughter at the highest level.

On one particular afternoon while Kellie was at school, I was sitting in front of the TV in my yellow Queen Anne's chair when a voice in my head kept saying to me, "Get up and get to work. You promised God you would write a book or an article to increase income." After ten minutes of this nagging, I got up and climbed the stairs to my office. At that very moment, a bullet came through the window across the room and went directly into the headrest of the chair where I had been sitting. It punctured the precise space my head would have been had I remained sitting there.

When the police arrived, they determined the gun was shot by the man who lived behind us doing target practice in his backyard. They told me that had I been sitting in that chair, I would be dead.

From that time on, I remained more conscious of those times God was recruiting me for His purposes and tried to do my best to hear His call. Any time I needed additional motivation, I thought about the day that the police told me if I had not moved at the moment I did, keeping my agreement with God, I would be dead.

Our relationship with God in faith is a two-way street—we cannot ask for help from Him without being available to render help when called upon.

Fifteen

God Meets Our Needs in Unexpected Ways

Several verses of the Bible promise that those who have faith and obey the Word need not fret about their human needs. On many occasions, I have experienced the ever-presence of that promise to meet all my needs.

Building a business from the ground up is a challenge that requires total trust that God is your employer. Armed with a book on public relations, stamps for fifty mailings, and the knowledge I had gained as a news reporter, I set out to build a business that would enable me to finance my daughter's college degree.

Public relations work entails promoting clients or products through electronic or print media in order to increase exposure. It is also used to sell an idea or philosophy to a targeted group of people. Both of these tasks, if well executed, will earn more money for clients or get them elected to the office they seek.

There were times when my daughter and I had no disposable income and very few of the basics we needed to survive. Just before Labor Day, I completed a large PR project for a client that would net us two months of financial security. I looked forward to a healthy chunk of income. I'd earmarked some money for a movie and perhaps a burger at McDonald's. I was anxious to receive the promised check in the mail, making several trips to the mailbox. This was Friday afternoon, and I needed to deposit the check before the banks closed for the long weekend. With each passing hour, my fear grew. The client had not kept his word. By 4:30, I felt compelled to call their office and offer to pick up the check. The banks closed at 6:00, and after that I would be out of money for the entire three-day weekend.

When I called, I was told by the secretary that the office was closed for the holiday weekend, and no one was there who could help me. I was panicked. Our cupboards were almost bare, and I had little cash for food. Kellie was old enough by then to discern a real problem. Above all else, I did not want her to feel insecure.

I got on my knees and prayed. I reaffirmed my hope and trust that God was always with us and that, as always, I was working for Him. "You are my boss." Prayer and trust did not reduce my anguish, however. I had a terrible fear I'd have to ask the church or friends for a meal. Thus far, my rule had been not to ask anybody for anything. I was self-sufficient, demonstrating God's abundance to me. With each hour, I felt more distress. As the time approached for the banks to close, I felt near hysteria, repeating the 23rd Psalm aloud over and over.

By 6:00, an hour beyond the time I had expected the check to arrive in the mail, I was brokenhearted and mulling over what to do next. The doorbell rang. When I answered the door, a distinguished, suited gentleman stood there.

"Would you be interested in renting your garage?" he asked. "I see it's empty."

"I hadn't considered it, but it's a possibility," I said.

"It's at the side of the property, and I won't be in and out," he told me. "I would like to store my car and come by once a week to use it."

"Do you live around here?" I asked.

"I'm Mrs. Cox's son from next door. I just came to town to take a new job. I'm willing to pay $350 a month."

"I will rent to you." My heart smiled; relief washed over me—for an instant—until I remembered my bank was closed on Saturday. He reached in his pocket. "Sorry, will you take cash? Apparently, I've misplaced my checkbook."

This was one of so many instances when our needs were met in the most unexpected ways. Another incident that stands out as the absolute work of God was when my daughter was headed to UCLA. To my astonishment, she had graduated from high school at age fifteen. By her sixteenth birthday, she would be entering college because of her academic status. I was not ready for the transition either financially or emotionally. But I could not hold her back.

I was standing by the mailbox awaiting a very large payment due for a magazine story. This would take care of the deposit on my daughter's dorm room. The day before she was to leave for the university, I had bitten my nails to nubs, and my nerves were frayed. The check had not arrived. Where would she lay her head on her first night there if I didn't get them the deposit? I suppose some folks would have advised that I budget more wisely and save more money. I was doing my personal best as a single mom.

As I focused on washing the dishes to drown out my thoughts of whom I could borrow from, for some strange reason my good friend Chris dropped by unannounced. She said she came to say good-bye to Kellie. She and I had known each other more than eighteen years. She was a wonderful woman with a sweet heart, sensitive to everything around her. Her daughter was going to begin university with my daughter.

Chris said, "I know it costs a lot to put your daughter in university dorms, and you're all alone. I've been thinking; why don't I give you this and you can pay me back if or whenever you get extra cash." I looked down at the number written on the check—$1,000. It was the answer to my prayer. It would cover gas for the drive down to Kellie's Los Angeles college and back, lunch, and her dorm deposit. One thousand dollars was the number that puzzled me. How could she have known how desperate I was? Only God could have known because that was the number I had prayed for. My client's check arrived the day after my return from UCLA, and I repaid my friend, but God's generous timing was everything.

Another example of God meeting my needs is how He provided places to live despite the tedious process of looking. As I mentioned earlier, for an African American, house hunting even here in California can sometimes be overwhelming. Racism is rampant. Sometimes I have had a white friend follow up after I've been turned down just to find out what was really at work. After I've been turned down, the landlord is welcoming, and the apartment or house is available to my white friends.

One agonizing experience of this house-hunting trap that I endured happened just after a lengthy article appeared in the Sunday edition of the local newspaper, covering how I had been chosen Woman of the Year. I saw a condo I thought suited our needs. I called ahead to say I was a young woman, a businesswoman, and a single mother with a daughter.

When I arrived, the woman who opened the door first had a smile, and then a familiar scowl came over her face. "You speak beautiful English," she said. What she really meant was, "I couldn't tell you were black on the phone." Then her expression changed back to a smile as she recognized me from the newspaper article.

She invited me in for tea. She questioned me about my accolades and achievements and then, with that same gusto and enthusiasm, said she was sorry, but the condo had been rented during the hour between my phone call and my arrival. When I left, I was angry because she had wasted at least a half hour of my time in answering her questions.

I called Elana, a white friend, who was waiting down the street, standing by to do a follow-up. Sure enough, when she spoke with the landlady, the apartment was available. The same landlady urged her to apply and promised she could move in right away.

In the process of apartment or house hunting, I have several times collected enough evidence to sue but have never done so. I always trusted in the Lord that I'd find a home and a landlord who would welcome me with a smile. It has meant I have had to start the moving process earlier than most people; I must expect it will take me longer to find this smiling landlord.

Some of these encounters are more complex. I was heart-broken when the deed of one California house I purchased read, "No Negroes can ever own or reside in this house or this neighborhood." I called the real estate people, and the woman who answered said it was not their fault. The ban had been in place for years and years. She said it was just a tradition and that I should let it go—and I did. I decided it was merely words on a paper. The fact was I now owned the house. No matter how much the neighbors complained, they couldn't kick me out.

Through my faith and obedience to God's plan to meet all my needs, my housing needs have been fulfilled. Take, for example, my latest house. I had looked at forty-four places prior to running into this one. Houses in California at reasonable prices are as rare as hen's teeth, but much rarer for those with skin of color. Competition is ferocious no matter who you are.

I came upon an advertisement describing a lovely house with a view. The broker had urged me to come immediately. I was the first one to see the house. I was surprised to see a pleasant expression on the rental agent's face and no judgment in that smile in response to my color. It was extraordinary to me. Because I was tired of looking, I said to the woman, "I'll take the house now." It was dusk, the curtains were closed across the panel of windows, and I did not want to take the time to go through the downstairs. As people were lining up behind me, I just wanted to sign on the dotted line.

The rental agent who represented the management company was kind and sympathetic. She said, "I do not know how the landlord would feel about this." She was hesitant. "I am supposed to check with him on any nonwhite," but she would take the risk. She turned out to be a real angel. She signed me up without getting back to the landlord. Once she signed the contract on the owner's behalf, I felt secure.

Indeed, within a few days, the landlord did demand to see me. He claimed the house was not rented because he had not approved the agent's choice. He protested by asking for a larger deposit, which I gave him. Then he threatened to have the agent fired. Fearing he would destroy her career, I offered to relinquish the house to save her job. She, however, was willing to walk away from her job because she wanted me to have the house. I prayed; she insisted we remain.

On the fifth day of these discussions, I returned to the house and opened the curtains. For the first time, I saw an extraordinary view of the countryside, the bay, and the city that inspired me. I knew the space and the view would nurture our family. They would become an inspiration for all the love we could muster. My need for housing had been met.

It has been my experience that there is no free lunch. We are all responsible to work. A productive work ethic is our responsibility, but when there is a glitch and you have faith, all needs are met.

God meets our needs, sometimes in unexpected ways, when we have faith in God as our boss—our protector and provider.

Sixteen

AGE IS JUST A NUMBER

The early 1990s were an exciting and comfortable time in my life. For the first time, Kellie and I were enjoying abundance. We had developed a good relationship with our church, and we attended every Sunday and often extra activities on weekdays. By 1994, I had earned most of my higher academic degrees and written a critically acclaimed book, *Warriors Don't Cry*. Kellie was doing well in her university studies, and I had founded a successful public relations business.

Kellie had recently left for school. I was lonely for her company and the role of mother. I also felt I had too much time on my hands; there must be something more of value for me to do beyond writing, promoting my book, socializing, and working day and night.

I meandered through obligatory committees, church duties, and nonprofit fund-raising galas, but I felt lost. I was not really contributing. I was not doing what Grandma called God's work. I tried desperately to figure out what that might be. I felt so lonely and disconnected that I filled the void with meaningless busywork.

Not a day went by that I did not pray for the son, Christopher, I had lost at birth so long ago. Mother had said repeatedly there is no loss in God's universe. For everything taken, you will receive much more than you ever anticipated in return.

It felt as though I had climbed to the top of a mountain once more, but was it the wrong mountain? Now what? I missed the struggle to achieve, the stress of the professional climb, and especially, I missed being Mom. Friends called me a workaholic as I continued to make lists with ten things still to do. I had faith, but it needed renewal.

One day, I sat in front of the TV, staring at the screen, feeling lost. Suddenly, a face came on the screen that looked very much like my daughter, Kellie. I walked closer to the TV, hypnotized by the face that reminded me of her. I could not contain myself—rushing to the phone, I called to ask for information on the child being offered for adoption.

The person on the other end gasped when I answered her age question by saying, "I am turning fifty on December 7."

"You cannot qualify," the voice said.

"You're wrong," I replied. "Send me the paperwork," I demanded. "I have studied law for a year. I know all my rights."

Her answer startled me. "It's not one child; it's a set of three-year-old twins," she cautioned. "Would you split them up or keep them together? At your age, can you afford to raise two toddlers?"

I filled out the application, and over the next six months, I was concerned about qualifying. I did not mention my application to my daughter, who was attending college in Los

Angeles. I went on with my stodgy, robotic life. Then one day I got a call from the agency telling me they had completed the elimination process and four families had qualified. I was one of the four. "We want you to court."

"Court?" I asked. "What does that mean?"

"It means you show up in three days at this address bringing toys you've purchased for the boys."

I don't know whether I was serious or just kidding myself and God about this adoption. But the reality of seeing these children stressed me and paralyzed me with fear. Couldn't I have another five days or a week? Instead, they said I would meet in three days with the current foster mother, "who will introduce you to the children."

I asked God, "What am I doing? Is this crazy? Please show me which way to go. All my friends say I should not."

A social worker arrived to question me. She introduced herself by saying her husband said hello. I had worked with him as an intern at a CBS television station during the year I was at San Francisco State University. I accepted his wife's visit as a positive signal from God that I should move ahead with the adoption.

So I went toy shopping. I was truly taken aback by the prices. The price of toys had quadrupled since I had purchased toys for my now grown-up Kellie. I collected two little Polaroid cameras and two trucks and prepared myself to go and see the boys who might possibly become my sons.

I fell in love with them at first sight. They were like tiny, matching teddy bears, the most gorgeous teddy bears. They were so sad, so dear, and so lost. With a Russian mother and an African American father, they had an exotic appearance. They were much like little old men, edgy, savvy, and a bit rambunctious. They were almost four and had changed foster homes four times. They were aware another change was coming, that they were being looked over, and they looked me over too. Then they asked, "Why are you talking to us? Adults never talk to us." By the end of the visit, they had my heart. I wanted to take them home, never mind the other three families who had qualified.

I was on edge in the days that followed, praying constantly for the opportunity to raise them. Three visits later, I was told by a social worker I had never met before that I was a new mother. When that word came over the telephone, I was more frightened and more joyful than I could remember. I could hear Grandmother's words in my head: "Age is just a number. It is not God who attaches labels to us. It is we who burden ourselves with the stereotype linked to numbers."

In the beginning, many church members rejected me and my boys, saying how content they were to be empty-nest parents. The more time I spent with people who told me I should give the boys back, the more grateful I was for the new energy and purpose in my life. I lost a lot of friends who complained of their toddler exuberance and noise.

I replaced friends by spending time with Barney, Shari Lewis and Lamb Chop, and Mr. Rogers and his neighborhood, all members of the Public Broadcasting Network. I also began to network with the young parents at the playground and at my twins' school. All my days became new, fresh, and wonderful as I resurrected my mom instincts and learned to collect delicious hugs and tiny, wet kisses. I was so in love that I felt reborn.

With all the education and experience raising Kellie that I had attained by that time, I was able to address their upbringing with dedication and time and without panic. Still, in no way had I anticipated the energy it would take to raise four-year-old twins; least of all could I have anticipated that I would have to consult a therapist to learn that speaking to boys was different from speaking to girls. Yes, boys are different from girls in their thought patterns, even at the earliest stage.

For a time, my life was full of household chores, chasing my boys around, and keeping them in order. I would fall into bed with them before 9:00, totally exhausted. I thought to myself, *There must be some place in heaven for me because this is truly God's most challenging and robust work.* Now I understood why God did not usually give toddlers to older people to rear.

Adoption was a life-changing experience. Because of expenses with my boys for therapy and readjustment to family life and their need for private schools, I needed to seek other employment. I became a part-time professor and began earning my doctorate in International Multicultural Education at age fifty-five by going to weekend classes. As a result of that degree, I became a full-time professor. As the boys grew older, I was able to invest in their education and launch their lives. By the publication of this book, they will both be college graduates.

Adopting my twins made me a better Christian, a better teacher, and a better human being. Raising them was a daunting task that tested every aspect of my personhood while providing growth experiences for my body, mind, and spirit. It was an undeniable gift from God.

Not a day goes by that the words of the Bible don't come to mind: "The LORD gave, and the LORD hath taken away;

blessed be the name of the LORD" (Job 1:21 KJV). I still think of the son I lost more than fifty years ago, but now I also love two images of what he might have been like. I see the twins as God's gifts, a restoration of the loss I had suffered with the death of Christopher. It is a wonderful opportunity to nurture two of God's souls.

It took spiritual, physical, and mental growth for me to have the capacity to raise my young men in a way that will give them what they need to compete in the world. They bring forth the best from me and the highest gifts I can endow them with. I pray I have raised my young men to be children of God, Jesus's disciples.

People point to the fact that my financial situation and health might be better today had I not adopted. I respond to them, "There is nothing to replace the joy, peace, and pride I have in my sons."

"The LORD gave and the LORD has taken away; may the name of the LORD be praised." (NIV)

Seventeen

GOD IS AS CLOSE TO YOU AS YOUR SKIN

The Presidio of San Francisco offers a vast area of recreation that is extraordinarily beautiful. Its expansive walking path lined with sand dunes stretches seemingly forever along the many views of the bay, which glistens as it rolls out to meet the gray-blue skyline. Sparkling boats with water skiers following and extraordinary ships in the distance paint a picture that cannot be captured in one visit.

On this particular morning, I was taking my five-year-olds, Matty and Evan, for a long walk. It would be a family memory I would hold in my heart forever. They were so happy, pointing out the boats off in the distance and kicking the sand in the path with the toes of their shoes. As they darted back and forth, their glee was almost out of control.

Devoid of people for the most part, the area was splendid in its cleanliness and the pristine way its wooden benches and fauna emerged when one needed them. The one aspect of this trip that made me nervous was people who brought their dogs for a walk and thought it an appropriate place to unleash them.

As a young professor in my thirties and forties, I had walked this pathway a hundred times and enjoyed the scenery with no concern about the animals I saw. But now at age fifty-two, I moved slower and had my twin boys with me. Those dogs seemed much more treacherous because some of them were so much bigger than the twins were.

As the boys circled around me, running at breakneck speed and tumbling in the sand, I warned them repeatedly to stay within my sight. Suddenly, there appeared a dog that caught my attention because of his great size. I wondered whether it was a Great Dane or an Irish Wolfhound but decided on Great Dane because of its short brown hair. I felt my heart start beating rapidly. As I got closer, I saw the dog was even larger than I imagined. He was the size of a small pony.

"Matty, Evan," I called out loud. I wanted to get them and get away as quickly as possible. I wanted to feel their little hands in my hands. All of a sudden, Evan was skipping toward the dog with his right hand up to greet it. I screamed at him, "Evan, stop!" Then I heard the voice of the owner coming from my right side saying, "Lady, stop. Tell your son to stop. Dante has been trained to hunt and destroy. Be careful. Don't move. Stay absolutely still."

What did he mean by that? I had to get my son Evan.

"Lady, grab your other son by the hand and put your hands at your sides and don't move."

I saw the man inching toward the dog, giving him hand signals and speaking in a quiet voice. I could hear the dog growl and bark with a loud, deep bark. His bark frightened

Evan, and he began to scream and cry. "Lady," the man said to me calmly, "he should not show fear to that dog. Listen to me, please. This is an emergency."

I couldn't think what to do next. I wondered why the owner did not command the dog to come to him. I was feeling a sense of panic with tears falling down my face. Matthew was feeling panic and whimpering while holding my hand tightly. I pondered what to do next, and I thought back to the first weeks I had gotten them—now almost a year ago. I had enrolled them in Sunday school, and we had done morning readings. We had talked daily about how strong and powerful Jesus is and how He is here now. I thought about the statement that my grandmother had constantly repeated when I was a child growing up. "God is as close to you as your skin, you have but to call out and He will answer, you have but to ask and He will help you."

I realized right away I could not spread my panic to either one of the boys. I swallowed my fear and began speaking in a very low voice. I said to Evan, "Do you see Jesus? He's right there beside you, son. See the beautiful waves and the sun on the flowers? Jesus must be right there. That is His beauty, His ocean, His sky. Oh, Evan, aren't we lucky? Jesus is taking a walk with us."

I paused to lower my voice even one more notch. I wanted him to stop his panicked outcry to me and to remain still and calm even as the dog owner told him, "Be still and put your hands at your side." He was whimpering, his little, wrinkled face reflecting his fear.

I couldn't think of anything to do next. I choked down more panic and tears as I said to him, "Jesus likes the dog. See Him smiling? Everything is going to be okay."

He took a breath and looked around. "Where, Mama?"

"He's right there beside you. Remember, I told you He brought you and me together, and He will always be with us."

"But, Mom!"

"No, Evan, look at the doggie. Isn't he beautiful? Don't pet him now, just stand with Jesus and look at him."

"He's here?"

"Yes, Evan, He's there."

"Mom, Mom, you come now."

"No, give me a moment, but stop crying and show Jesus how brave you are and how much you are enjoying His visit."

Matthew stopped crying and looked up at me questioning. "Jesus came on the walk too? Do we have enough lunch for Him?"

"Jesus always has lunch. Remember the fishes and the loaves of bread? We are all okay."

Evan began to fret again. "Mom, come. Why can't I come to you?"

Between my son and that big dog there were mounds of sand. They were about twenty feet apart with smaller mounds between them. The owner was about twenty feet away to the left. Other people were beginning to gather around, talking of calling the police. Some of them had seen the dog previously and said he was a real danger.

Suddenly, as I said aloud, "God in heaven, show me what to do next," one of the mounds of sand began to move. My eyes were riveted to the sight. It was a man, a bum with dirty clothes, a grungy face, and a beard. First he stretched, then he stood up, walked over to the dog, grabbed his collar, and walked him over to his owner where he said, "Man, you should do a better job handling your dog." Then he turned and called out to me, "Lady, get your boy. This is one place where you have to keep him close to you because there are some vicious dogs out here."

"Oh, my Lord, thank You so much." I rushed over to Evan and picked him up and hugged him tight. Then I said to the man, "Thank you so much. What can I do for you? Can I give you cash for lunch or the lunch I have in this bag?"

He said, "No, Lady, no, no. The Lord Jesus provides everything I need every day. I just need a nap." Turning to the crowd that had gathered, he said, "The show's over." The crowd started to disperse.

For a long moment, I stood still and thought, *Jesus came with us on this walk, and it is really important for my children to know that Jesus is always with them, just like Grandma said.*

I knew my boys would have to learn what Grandma had taught me, which is to walk by faith and not by sight alone. This experience was the first step in teaching them that no matter what threatening evidence appears to be true, we need not fear because God is always beside us.

Eighteen

OUR NIGHTMARE
DREAM HOUSE

My now seven-year-old twins and I were house hunting. After more than six weeks of being turned down because I was African American or because I had children or because, because—lo and behold, there before us was our dream home. We stared from outside the front gate, and I cautioned the boys not to dare to hope for this castle, which was obviously far beyond our budget.

Located in a most secretive area of lush Marin County, California, it was a mansion, a castle, far beyond my dreams. My real estate agent said, "Oh, take a chance. Step in and take a look! I have the key to the lockbox right here. It is far above your budget, but the owner is a bit anxious right now. Let's make an offer if you really like it."

I stepped through the gold, wrought-iron gate, and there before me was paradise. It looked like something from a movie about the rich and famous. It had double stained-glass doors at the entryway, sequestered below an overhanging second-floor balcony with a black and gold banister. The exterior of the building had been done in a rare Brazilian hardwood at an unmentionable price. According to Gina, the realtor and my good friend, it took an entire army of professionals to take care of the wood in this place. My inclination had been not to go one step farther, as I knew I could not afford it. Once again, Gina urged me forward, saying, "Miracles do happen, Melba. Don't you believe in miracles?"

"Of course, I do, but I don't believe they come in this form."

I do trust Jesus to guide me, I thought to myself. *For certain I do.*

"I suppose there is no harm in taking a look." My seven-year-olds were restless, ready to explore what seemed to be our dream house. The house was a stunning configuration of circles. The front of it looked like a semicircle with the sun bouncing off the glossy, Brazilian wood exterior. The roof was a dome like a Russian church, glistening even more in the sunlight.

Once inside the front hallway, we could see the entire house was filled with sunlight. I was overwhelmed by the surrounding deck doors and gigantic windows. As I looked up the two stories through a circular staircase, high up through the third story to the dome to the sky, I saw that three-quarters of the entire roof was glass. The second story was filled with four oversized bedrooms that surrounded a balcony in the center.

As the tour progressed, we saw the circular kitchen with its glossy, black granite counters and cupboards all framed in Brazilian wood to match the outside. The appliances were done in stainless steel. I felt I was continuing into a movie that began outside at the front gate. The enormous size and amazing, unique décor took my breath away. The house was beyond anything I had ever seen outside the movies.

Peering through the circular window in the living room, I saw it—a black onyx pool. The boys were running wild up the circular stairwell toward the second-floor bedrooms, none of them smaller than eighteen by twenty feet. The master suite was the size of a moderate apartment with a sunken Jacuzzi tub done in pink marble. I kept standing still and staring. The realtor had to grab my arm and drag me forward from each stop.

Suddenly, the realtor had changed her stance to a more formal one and was smiling at someone in the hall just outside the master suite. The smiling, petite Asian woman, the owner who had happened to drop by, came into the room and extended her hand to me. It seemed as though she had magically and silently appeared in a bubble of jewels and St. Laurent. Her face was beautiful with a smooth complexion. It was the deeply entrenched frown lines in her forehead that revealed the great stress she must have been under.

"How do you like it?" she asked.

I replied, "Oh, it's beautiful. Far more than anything I could imagine."

"If you were to move in, I would want to be assured that the boys could treat the home with respect."

"Oh yes," I responded, "I've taught them that one must be committed to respecting one's environment because it exemplifies respect for one's self."

"By the way, what do you do for a living? Do you give wild parties?"

"No, ma'am," I said. "I am a Christian woman, the mother of two babies and a grown-up daughter. Now, in my fifties, I spend most of my time going to church, taking care of the children's education, and writing. I'm thinking about going back to school to earn another doctorate degree."

"You don't smoke."

"I don't, and I don't drink."

"Oh, come have a seat. You are just who I'm looking for. I want more than anything else a tenant who will protect this house until I come back from Asia. I'll rent it to you for half price. What are you?"

"I'm an African American."

"Your boys don't look African American. They have blond hair around the temple edges and golden-brown head hair, not at all the features of an African American."

"Although with all the diversity going on, African Americans can look almost any way these days," I said. "In my case, I adopted them a few years back."

"All right," she said. "The neighbors won't necessarily applaud the African American identification."

Even at half price, her $3,000 cost per month was over the top of my budget. But after much prayer and meditating, I thought this was a miracle blessing being offered by God because I'd been such an angel. Surely he could provide opportunities to earn extra money—like tutoring or writing ad copy, which I had done in the past. Before long, we were moved in and bathing ourselves in the splendor of it all.

It was heavenly—a real home that I felt was perfect for the boys and my grown-up daughter racing to carve a career for herself. The boys could walk back and forth to school through a safe neighborhood on their own. We found welcoming neighbors.

One morning a few weeks after settling in, as I walked about the backyard meditating and praying, the gardener greeted me with a stressed expression.

"Madam, I hate to show you this, but I feel you have a problem."

He led me to the rear of the house and pointed out one of the family room windows. The screen was torn, and there were scrape marks all over the window sill—some of which dug deep into the wood—and damage to the window frame on all sides. I was stunned. It frightened me. Was someone trying to break into my house while we were sleeping? My bedroom was a story above this spot. What should I do?

I phoned the police, and they came right over. The combination police and fire department station was less than two blocks away. That information did make me feel a bit better, but they confirmed my greatest fear—someone had attempted to enter our home. When? And why? Those were the two questions I mulled over with Kellie. In one instant, the police had asked whether this was something the boys would do. However, without questioning them, they decided they were neither tall enough nor strong enough and not vicious enough.

Kellie and I concluded we would not discuss this matter with the boys. We already had a front door alarm that we seldom used because of its complexity. The police suggested we get a baby monitor to place downstairs in the front hallway with the listening device in our rooms to help us hear activity from the living room and the rear of the house, both of which were far away from our second-floor bedrooms. To say we were frightened was an understatement. It reminded me of my childhood when I feared the Ku Klux Klan or worried an individual would come and hurt us or take Mother or Grandmother away.

An entire month passed, and I certainly wasn't living as though life were business as usual. I felt threatened and less comfortable in the home I had so treasured, especially when I was alone. I was even suspicious of the carpenter and painters the landlord sent to fix the window.

One bright, sunny Sunday afternoon about a month later, the boys and I had gone to attend a dance theater performance my daughter participated in. We returned to the house at dusk. As I entered the front gate, it seemed eerie, and I immediately felt uncomfortable. Curtains were blowing out of all the upper-deck doors. But how could that be? I had locked all the deck doors both downstairs and on the second floor. Nevertheless, as we drew near to the front door, we could see the deck doors were all standing open, and the front door was also ajar an inch or two.

As I stepped across the threshold, my heart was pounding in my chest. I heard rustling in the back of the house. Then there was the breathtaking slam of the back door. I could see that the part of the house in my view was totally torn apart. It was astonishing! We grabbed the boys, backed out, and ran for the car. I called the police on my cell phone. They were there in an instant. Swarming about the house, they called in an additional gentleman who began taking pictures and brushing everything with a fine black powder.

As I moved about, I could see the house was torn apart from the top floor, which housed my tiny writing office, down to the first floor and even the garage and storage room. Nothing was in place—everything was torn off shelves and strewn about. It had taken us hours and hours of work to organize and distribute our possessions, and now what would we do?

"These persons were obviously searching for something specific," the policeman in charge said. "Do you have any idea what they were seeking?"

"We do not," I replied as my wounded mind frantically searched my memory.

"No, no, why—we don't have anything anybody would covet," Kellie whispered, sadness and fear painting her face.

Kellie and I could see that the uniformed police and their swarm of activity made the boys very nervous. They had been working on a special science project for weeks. It devastated them to find the fine black dust all over their work. Tears streaming down their cheeks, they finished their bowls of chicken soup and put on their pajamas. They went to bed by 8:30 without any coaxing. I had to get them up to get on their knees for our prayer time.

"Can Jesus make the robbers go away?" Evan asked.

"There is nothing Jesus cannot do, and we are going to pray unceasingly that He will always protect us." They managed slight smiles and snuggled down on their pillows. We all were exhausted and frightened by 9:00 p.m. when the police finally left.

My heartbeat was fast and furious as I raced around the house checking window and door locks and covering windows with sheets that I had previously left uncovered with a casual attitude of safety and comfort. I experienced a feeling I had never felt before—that of knowing for certain that someone had been in my home, an uninvited stranger about whom

I knew nothing and who knew absolutely nothing about all of us. It was clear to Kellie and me that the robbers had taken away what was most precious to us—the safety and sanctity of home. We were suddenly not so thrilled by the beautiful home; it was now perhaps an unsafe and temporary shelter.

I didn't sleep at all that night, and neither did Kellie. The next morning, one of the female police officers came to talk to us. She informed us that we should take certain precautions—one might be to learn to use the house alarm efficiently and to purchase a device that would allow us to hear what was happening on the first floor at all times of the night. She pointed to the glass doors, floor-to-ceiling deck doors, and huge windows that made us very vulnerable. Following her visit, I felt as though we were living in a glass house and anyone could throw stones at any time. I felt nude.

It was a week before we felt comfortable sleeping even for a small portion of the night. Our schedules changed—no movies, no late-evening school meetings, no going to the library, despite the fact that both Kellie and I were working on doctoral degrees. We didn't leave home at night, and we began a process of lockup and windows check at dusk that seemed to go on forever.

During the daylight hours, the huge, beveled-glass skylights, the stained-glass door with its sparkling colors, and the very wide, tall windows ceased to be beautiful. Instead, they were points of entry by a stranger who could be dangerous. The entire dynamic of our family changed to a focus on fear. Taking the next step to protect ourselves dominated our conversation and our time.

Less than a month later, we came home from our various schools to find the gardener pointing to all the windows at the rear of the house, which had been jammed with a sharp object. The wood frame of the windows had been seriously damaged. So we called the police to see what should be our next step. They came right over and confirmed that someone had tried to enter the rear of our home. Had it happened while we were at school or the night before? Pondering "when and why" robbery questions became my obsession.

The police asked that we immediately telephone the landlady to find out whether the rear glass windows were wired to the alarm system or just the front door, because it was seen as a real help in fending off robbers. The police suggested the landlady wire the rear windows. Within a week, that process began. Still, even the presence of the installers made me nervous.

We asked our church members to pray for us. We increased our Bible reading to ensure our trust and faith remained strong. Still, to feel vulnerable in the place we should be the safest is unexplainable in words. The interior of this wonderful castle became like a torture chamber. I began praying day and night, pleading with Jesus to help me rebuild my hope and joy and faith.

Months passed, and we kept in touch with the police. They questioned the landlord about whether she knew of anyone who sought something she had in that home. As Christmas approached, I noted we had all become nervous wrecks, frightened to stay at home, frightened to go out for any reason after dark, and reluctant to leave home at any time of the day. I feared being left home alone as I had been in the months before when I worked from home. I sought ways to find peace and to share that peace with my children.

That led me to read the Bible each morning and evening and to form habits that included the family in my praying.

Since the house was constructed with all bedrooms on the second floor, placed around a circular balcony, one could stand outside their bedroom or the three bathrooms on that floor and look down to the first floor below. There were very high ceilings and, thus, many stairs going down from the second to the first floor. Along the railing of that balcony, the builder had placed a flower box, which I took joy and pride in filling with potted plants as Grandmother had taught me earlier in my life.

On one particular evening, enough time had passed since our last incident that I had gone to bed after checking and rechecking doors, window locks, and every possible entry. I even sat on the stairs and stared for a time high up at the skylight far above us, wondering whether one could climb up to the roof, crack the dome, and enter that way. I concluded no human could endure the twenty-two-plus-foot drop from that glass dome to the balcony floor.

Once in bed, I lay awake for a long time before I fell asleep. I was awakened by the opening of the heavy glass deck door. Heart thumping, I rushed to the balcony to peer over and saw curtains being blown inward by the chill wind of the winter night. I rushed around the circle and into Kellie's room.

"Shhhh—Mom, quiet down. It's all right, you're hearing things."

"No, no, no, Kellie, please."

She followed me out of the room and went into my bedroom to call the police, while I continued to bend over the railing of the balcony. And there he was, a crisply dressed, brown-haired man who looked up at me.

Our eyes met, and when he made no effort to turn and run, I knew I was in trouble. I began yelling and ran to grab the phone from Kellie to tell the police to hurry. The woman on the other end, whose voice sounded familiar, said, "Now, Melba, calm down—please don't have a heart attack. They will be there in a moment."

When I went back to peer over the railing, the man was climbing the stairs with a butcher knife in his hand. My brother, who had spent his life as a policeman and US Marshall, had told me, "Once your attacker comes near, you have lost the battle. Never ever let them near."

"Please help me, Jesus, please, please . . ."

That's when my eyes fell on the clay pots filled with flowers I had so carefully planted. Instinctively, I reached for them and began to toss them down. So there Kellie and I stood, tossing my beloved pots down the stairs into the face of our would-be robber, who appeared stunned by our actions. We tossed as hard as we could as we screamed at him like madwomen. At first, he seemed determined to come up, but a few hits by pots filled with damp dirt and the rain of cracked-clay-pot debris caused him to stop and think for a moment. The boys had bravely joined us, flinging their toys down at him.

After what seemed like forever but was only a few minutes, two policemen arrived. There they were outside the stained-glass window, valued at $70,000, banging their fists on the door frame.

"Please, please," I screamed. "Don't! Don't! I'll let you in or, better, go around." The robber looked around and headed for the door he had apparently entered. The same one I was directing the police to enter. When the police came inside, we pointed them toward the robber, but they wanted a description and time to summon help—lots of help. There began a circus that would go on for the next two hours, whereby they would light up the neighborhood and mount the roofs of our neighbors. For those who had not been aware of "African Americans in the neighborhood," this was our now infamous introduction. "We're here!"

I would awaken at 3:13 every morning for the following year if not longer.

As Christmas drew near, we opened the small storage room adjoining the garage only to find all of our decorations and my papers dumped out on the floor. They were meticulously rummaged through as if, once more, someone knew exactly what they were looking for.

My prayers grew more frequent and longer as I focused on how we could find another home. More and more, I wondered how we could survive in an environment that was affecting my health and my hope. Still, the practical truth was that it cost thousands of dollars to move and many, many hours to find a place. Both Kellie and I were midway on our doctorates. Refiling and organizing the books and papers attendant to that move was unimaginable.

We decided if God was with us always, we would not be chased away by human invasion. We proceeded to practice contentment, even in that house and yard. Somehow, the quiet presence of Jesus's spirit and His promise of safety and harmony at home brought us peace. I posted sheets of paper on the front and back doors and the window the robbers had attempted to enter saying, "Please come in and take what you wish and enjoy it in good health. The door is unlocked. Please don't make a mess."

No one bothered us again in that house. We lived there for a year until a notion and a need directed us to move.

———————

Even in the face of my distraction with earthly beauty and pleasures and my overwhelming fear at the intruder, God remained with me, protecting me every moment.

Nineteen

TERROR TIMES TWO

My twins were rambunctious and always ready for adventure. Since I was working full-time as a professor by the time they were eight, I had to have a caregiver to get them off to school. One morning when I arrived at the university, my assistant, Grace, reminded me I had planned an exam for my first-class students. Checking my briefcase, I discovered I had left the exam at home. A university exam day is precious and not to be skipped for anything but an emergency.

I told Grace that if she would take over the first fifteen minutes of my class and have students discuss the news of the day, I would rush home to get the exam.

I arrived home to find my nine-year-olds being ushered out the front door to a blue Lexus convertible by a strange man I'd never seen before.

"Where are you going?" I asked.

"Thank you, Mom. We got the new puppy you sent," Evan shouted.

"Hi, Mom, school," Matthew said. "Our puppy is in the car."

"This is the man you sent to pick up the boys," Mary, my caregiver, explained from the doorway.

At this point, the man stared at me with a look of fear, jumped down the first three steps, ran to the car, and gunned his engine and sped away.

"Leave the puppy," the boys shouted.

"Hey, there! Who are you?" I screamed.

The boys spoke up, both at once, obviously disappointed. "That's the man that's going to get us a puppy. And give us a job walking his puppy after school."

"Where did you meet him?" I questioned.

"At school," Evan said.

"No, no, no, at Walgreens, over there," Matt said.

As the boys completed their story, I was hysterical inside, to say the least, but pretending all was well. I immediately called the police. When officers arrived, they knew of a similar situation not far from my house. They recognized the description of a tall man with a muscular build and a mustache. They referred to him as one of the "bears." I wondered why the officer referred to him as one of the bears as he was skinny.

Shortly afterward, they sent a team of officers, a man and a woman, from the sex crimes unit to the house. The woman separated the boys to interview them.

Although I had instructed them not to talk to strangers, not to take offers of candy or gifts from strangers, they were not prepared to deal with an offer of their own puppy and a paying job walking another puppy. They had not bothered to tell me about it as they hoped to make money for a birthday present for me. After lengthy questioning, they reported reluctantly that this man had been after them for a while.

Two hours later, I realized I had skipped exam day and two classes without even notifying Grace I wasn't coming back. My cell phone, left behind in the car, was clogged with calls and texts. From then on, my heart, head, and energy were focused on one thing only—protecting my sons. The police warned me that they did not have enough resources and men to guard my sons and me twenty-four hours a day. It would be up to me to arrange my life so that I knew where my boys were at all times of the day and night. It would be up to me to protect them.

Our lives became a living nightmare, full of stress and uneasiness. As nine-year-olds, the boys didn't want to spend all their time with their mother. My friends already called me "Smother Mother." Later on, I could look back and mark that day on my calendar as the beginning of a dreadful year, causing me to be overprotective.

First, I sat down and made a detailed schedule, as I needed to make provisions for someone I trusted to watch the boys when I couldn't. The routine made the boys as nervous as it made me, except they didn't quite understand why I was fearful. They were disturbed that they could no longer play alone with their friends.

In the days to come, we altered all our habits to ensure our protection. During the cool weather, I used to go for walks in the enclosed local shopping mall, which had a clearly defined play area with children's furniture and a food court. We would walk for a while and then settle into the food court and take advantage of the variety of restaurants.

On this particular day, I was sitting on a bench looking at the boys, who were standing fifty feet away ordering the food they had chosen for dinner. Suddenly, two large men moved in to sit on either side of me. They closely resembled Smokey the Bear, whom I often saw on television. They were tall, stocky, muscular, and wore beards. As they moved closer, their presence began to chill my mind, and their words—veiled threats—immersed me in fear.

"It's best you not disturb anyone or call the boys," the older one said. "May we have a moment of your time?"

"How can I help you?" I spoke calmly despite my hysteria.

"I understand you have had an incident and told the police about our friend's generous offer of a puppy the other day. We'd like to relieve you of that problem before it grows so big you can't handle it."

"Excuse me," I said, "what do you mean by that?"

He replied, "You don't really need to be discussing your issues with the police. We know your boys and want to see them safe. Such fine young men they are."

His smile brought burning anger to my entire being. "Why do you care what I do with my boys?"

"It would probably be in your best interest not to burden the police with your small and inconclusive issues. Best not to talk anymore about the ride and the dog-walking job your boys were offered."

"Why? How could it be in my boys' best interest?"

"It's in everyone's best interest. You'd keep them alive."

"Or, let's look at this problem another way," the younger one said. "You could probably use a house. We don't want to think of our professors renting. It's not a good role model. You're a renter, aren't you?"

The fear was burning through my body. How could I get from between these men, get my boys, and get out of there safely? What was I going to do? In the back of my mind, I knew I couldn't offend them. Should I call for help? Just shout "Help!"? Should I try to flag one of the policemen nearby?

"I don't understand," I said.

"You live in somebody's house near Walgreens. We are prepared to provide you with a residence that you would own. You could pick out new carpeting and choose the furnishings, right here in Mill Valley. We would take care of that. Your boys would be safe. Maybe we could even mentor them."

"I see," I said. Something told me not to get angry, threaten them, or say anything negative. They were too big. They still squeezed me between them, and I could feel their strength. Their arm muscles bulged. Their bodies looked as though they were chipped from concrete. They had chiseled, muscular faces, and one of them had dyed hair. Right away, it occurred to me they knew more about me than I knew about them. They knew my residence, my workplace, and more. I knew nothing about them. I was vulnerable. The police couldn't find them immediately, but they could find me.

"Don't talk to the police again. You must drop the matter." Then just as quick as the bears came, they stood and said, "We'll be in touch," then disappeared into the crowd.

I was shaking so badly yet paralyzed with fear. *Please, God, give me strength to collect myself and get my boys without frightening them.*

All I wanted then was to get myself and my boys out of there alive without alarming them. With my heart beating a thousand beats a minute, I rushed to the boys. I paid for their dinners, bagged the food, and hustled them to the car, which was parked in a dark, underground area. Fortunately, I had parked at the end where there was some light. Although I was very frightened, I couldn't let anyone know just how frightened I was. But the boys knew right away there was something the matter.

"Mom, what's wrong?" Matt said. "Why do we have to go now?"

They were fretting about leaving the mall as they had wanted a ride on the carousel before going home. I told them we couldn't miss a special TV show. I told them we must pray to ask God to come with us. So we prayed in the car. When they were five, I had begun a habit of praying every morning on their way to school. Now was the time to add the habit of afternoon prayer. From that day forward, every time we've gotten into the car, we've begun the trip with prayer.

As time passed, the bears came to the house and climbed the stairs to the front door and rang the bell to reemphasize their offer of a house if I kept my mouth closed. They called our house at midnight or 1:00 a.m. or 2:00 a.m.—whenever the mood hit them. They also followed us into church and to the barber shop. Meanwhile, I found myself in the middle of a major police investigation. The officers confiscated all our home computers and assigned a patrol car to drive by our house several times at night.

I kept wondering, *Why me, God?*

As the days rolled by, the boys became more restless in the confines of the house and car. Even when they went to their favorite places, I was with them, directly next to them.

The days turned into months, and I prayed harder and had peace of mind only when we were in church with our friends all around us. I could only confide in a few people who occasionally came to spend the night to guard us. Although I felt like we suffered forever, I had faith that God would care for us and guide us to safety and peace. Some days I cried in my car parked in the lot of the university. "Please, God, will we ever be free again?"

On one occasion on a Sunday afternoon, we went to a local grocery store, which I had changed to in order to avoid anyone tracking me. The boys had a habit of getting their own basket and veering away from me to collect their favorites. It was a huge store with many aisles. Soon the boys came running up to me and began dumping their purchases in my cart. They were pointing to the left and telling me the bears were over there. I collected them by my side, got in line, and proceeded to the checkout stand. As usual, one skittered away from my side for bubble gum and the other followed. Suddenly, the two bears approached. One got in front of me and one behind, between me and the boys.

Standing there amid all the customers checking out in the front of the grocery store, I knew I had to remain calm and knew God was right there, right then. The boys knew enough about the situation, because of police lectures, that they were distressed. They stopped bickering about gum and pushed their way past the men to me.

"Thought any more about that deed to a house with your name on it? The offer stands, you know."

I answered as calmly as I could. "Yes, it's very generous of you." I avoided eye contact as I looked down and stroked Evan's hair, since he was on the brink of tears.

It was time for the one in front of me to check out. "I'll be in touch," he said as he left, the second man trailing behind.

It was dusk when we got outside the store and headed for our car. All of a sudden, as I loaded the groceries into the trunk of the car, a bright light was in our faces. A car raced toward us, then screeched to a halt with the lights shining in our eyes. There was nothing I could do. Aloud I said, "Lord, have mercy on us!"

Six months later, the police tracked the predator down through the information on our computers. They knew his name and where he lived. They had his correspondence with the boys. He had been pretending to be another boy in another city and a member of their Scout group. He continuously invited them out. At that point, we realized God had been with us every step of the way.

The next day, the police told me they had arrested the predator and the two bears. A court date would be set, and the boys would need to testify. That worried me. We had to go to the police station several times, and several times the female police officer who had been with us from the beginning came to the house to interview the boys for court, to clarify events with the predator.

When the court date came, the twins were frozen with fear because they had never been on the witness stand before. They didn't want to go. When we got to court, the female officer was waiting for us. She took us into a room next to the courtroom and told us to have a seat. She'd be back when we were needed. As we waited, I prayed. I felt as though this event would unhinge me.

After about an hour, the officer returned to say the predator had pled guilty and that the boys' testimony was not necessary. After signing some papers, I took my boys' hands in mine and together we walked out of the building. Taking a deep breath, I got into the car and we prayed, "Thank You."

From that time forward, I have thanked God. There have been no more midnight phone calls, no more threatening cards. We have been safe.

———

As complex and dangerous as a predicament may be, God is as close as our skin. Although peril feels like forever, God is here now. He will guide us through the jungle of fear, if only we will listen and obey.

Twenty

WHERE THERE IS FAITH, THERE IS HOPE, FORGIVENESS, AND GRATITUDE

Tuesday, November 9, 1999

Washington, DC, the White House: *Is this really happening to me?* the voice in my head asked over and over. There I was walking down the hallway of the White House. President Clinton walked directly on my left and a throng of erudite statesmen surrounded me as we approached the Gold Room. I was there with the other members of the Little Rock Nine to receive one of our country's highest civilian awards, the Congressional Gold Medal. As we neared the wide, double-door entrance, our pace sped up, and the vast audience of dignitaries stood and applauded. We nine were allowed to bring ten of our family members and friends. It was a once-in-a-lifetime occasion. The snap of cameras filled the air, and photographers darted back and forth.

As I approached and mounted the steps to the stage, my feet hurt. I should never have worn brand-new shoes on this special day. The nine of us were lined up, filing to our seats behind President Clinton. We took our seats, and the beautiful music began. Thoughts raced through my head at the speed of light: *I can't believe I'm here in the White House, enjoying a reception in my honor, and receiving this country's highest medal for bravery.* For all of these many years, I had wondered if what I did back in 1957 by integrating Little Rock's all-white Central High School against all odds was wrong. It tore the social fabric of the community where I lived and divided us all into warring factions. It was a life-threatening fiasco that changed my life focus.

There in the Gold Room, I stood in a place that few Americans have stood. Fewer than three hundred Americans have received this noble honor, and yet within the hour I would be holding it in my hand. That was when it dawned on me that it was God's way of saying, "Melba, this extraordinary award is because you kept your faith, followed My directions, and completed My assignment in a manner that I hoped you would. You learned from My pilgrim, Dr. King, that your painful labor was not for yourself but for a generation not yet born."

The enthusiastic applause of the crowd pulled me back to reality. I settled into my seat and listened to the president begin his speech of gratitude to us Little Rock Nine for contributing to a historic and significant change in education.

My mind drifted back to the day I first heard I had been nominated for this honor. During the fortieth anniversary celebration of the Little Rock integration in 1997, we heard about a bill presented to Congress for us to receive a medal. Representative Ben Thompson of Mississippi and Arkansas

Senator Dale Bumpers had introduced it. We laughed because the article said Congress had to agree to vote it through. How likely was that?

The official call came in September. It was 1:30 in the afternoon. I was seated at my desk, writing an article for a magazine and watching the clock so I could go to school to pick up my twins. The routine was set in stone; I would pick them up, go to McDonald's for a Happy Meal, spend twenty minutes at the playground, weather permitting, and come home for our study time and an enjoyable evening.

The voice on the phone said, "Congratulations, Mrs. Beals. Do you know that Congress has voted yes on a bill to award you with the Congressional Gold Medal? What are you going to do to celebrate?"

"I'm going to McDonald's for a Happy Meal," I answered, sincerely thinking someone was teasing me.

"Would you give us your address? We want to come over and interview you?"

"The Congressional Gold Medal?" I asked.

"Yes."

"Sorry, I have to pick up my twins from school. If Congress agrees on something, it will be a great blessing. Call back when that happens," I said. I quickly went over to the encyclopedia to check on what the Congressional Gold Medal was. It seems that since the American Revolution, Congress has commissioned gold medals as its highest expression of national appreciation for distinguished achievements and contributions by individuals and institutions. When I read this, I nearly fainted. It is very special. Indeed, God had smiled on us even to have a bill presented, whether we actually received the medal or not.

"I'll never get that," I said as I scurried to meet my babies. "They are kidding. I can't be late to pick up my boys." Then my phone started ringing. I must have answered twenty calls before I went out the door.

When we returned home after our regular routine, the phone continued ringing off the hook with people asking for interviews, meetings, comments, and pictures.

I began to realize what that incredible medal meant. However, I put it in the back of my mind as the boys and I went about our daily routine. At one point, a reporter from a local television station came to the front door. One of the twins answered, and the reporter said, "Hi, I'm here to interview your mother."

My son said, "My mother, Melba, what for? She's just my mom. You must have the wrong house," and slammed the door.

Until that moment, I had been able to raise my children somewhat out of the limelight. I had deliberately avoided radio, newspapers, and television attention. I had made it a point not to let people know who I was because of its danger, and I was not looking for publicity for me or my children. There had always been threats looming overhead for our participation in Little Rock.

Now the cat was out of the bag. I was known to everyone. The next day, there were news vans in front of the house and parked in the driveway. None of my neighbors could miss this big event. I, on the other hand, was determined not to make a spectacle of myself and not to live in the spotlight with my kids.

As the days rolled on, we received further indications that it was not only possible but also probable that we would receive this award. In early October, a representative of the White House called and requested I submit names and social security numbers of the people I wanted to accompany me to the Gold Medal award ceremony. However, the reality of what was happening to me did not become clear until I was on a plane with my adopted mother, Kay McCabe, my sons, my daughter, and several friends landing at the Washington airport, preparing to go to the White House for the ceremony.

Now as I sat there and heard the president calling out names to hand each one of us the award, I was hypnotized by the enormity of the moment, the people there with me, the beautiful Gold Room, the White House photographer taking pictures, and the elegance of the ceremony. President Clinton called my name, handed me a small, open, green velvet box, and kissed my cheek. I whispered, "Thank You, God." Not for the incredible medal I held in my hand but for confirmation that faith, hope, forgiveness, and gratitude are God's keys to the grace that brought me to this place. *Thank You, Lord, for confirming that I followed Your directions—I am on the right journey.*

God speaks directly to us in many ways. And He confirms in many ways that we heard His direction and followed His requests.

Epilogue

On a beautiful Sunday afternoon in May, Mother's Day 2015, I sat staring off into the distance, feeling amazed and very grateful to be in such a welcoming and joyous environment. I was finally free of the hospital where I had been held prisoner by my ailing back for more than three months. In the background, I heard country rock music being played by the relatives of the famed rock group Grateful Dead. We sat in a restaurant and performance center called Terrapin Crossroads. It is a cozy place with music, the aroma of familiar food, and a milieu that reminds me of my Southern heritage.

Tears brimmed my eyes, and my heart felt as though I had been born again. I was surrounded by my twin sons and daughter, now adults, and family friends, who brought flowers and hugs and kisses to celebrate my rebirth.

Even though I was still in a wheelchair and still deep in a tediously long healing process, I was in awe of the power of God's blessings. At times over the past two years of pain, prayers, and rehabilitation, I wondered whether I would ever live to experience this enraptured scene. The voice inside whispered, *Be patient, it's happening—although you can neither see nor feel it, you're healing. Wait on the Lord, in His time.*

A sudden event had sucked me into a vortex of doctors, X-rays, powerful anesthetics, nurses, tiny dreary rooms, strange noisy beds, and white walls—a tunnel filled with loneliness. All that while, the taste of medicine permeated my mouth, and the punctured skin on my arms and legs ached. Above all else, I had lived through a reality fogged by endless drugs that seldom worked to rid me of the indescribable pain that plagued me day and night.

Two major spine surgeries within sixteen days became another opportunity for me to practice the dependence on faith in God stored up over my many years. Three operations in two years allowed me to replenish faith whittled down by loneliness and hospital rooms amid strangers. It was also a jolting opportunity for me to learn new and huge life lessons in relationships, patience, and humility, and in the power of silence, unconditional love, personal equality, and courage.

The long hospital stays were an unanticipated surprise! Like Grandma said, "Big surprises are special lessons from God—tests to see if you're paying attention—if you are listening to His instructions. Surprises are opportunities to renew your faith-building process."

This faith-building surprise began early in 2014. I had retired from my post as a university professor clutching my bucket list, with plans to take Tai Chi and piano lessons, have lunch with colleagues, shop with longtime sister/friends, spend long days writing fiction, read the great philosophers, increase my church activities, meditate, and maybe even earn another doctorate.

Within five months after retirement, during a regular visit to my orthopedist for a checkup, the surprise began. In a brief chat, I admitted I had fallen on my back and was now plagued by needle pricks all over my bottom. Immediately, he directed me to report to the University of California at San Francisco Hospital Spine Unit for X-rays. I would later learn that the pricks indicated urgent signals from my spine that it needed attention. I was stunned when, following the X-rays, I was hustled over to see a surgeon. Right away, he asked what I was doing that afternoon and urged me to have a spine operation immediately. Through tears of astonishment, I protested. He insisted that if I didn't comply immediately, I would be incontinent and confined to a wheelchair within six months.

Following six hours of surgery, I awakened in the Intensive Care Unit—feeling barely alive. I lay in shock, like a zombie, barely functioning. Over the next several days, I became exhausted of bedpans, tubes in my neck, and soup through straws. I was elated a few days later when the nurses unhooked me and allowed me to sit on a real toilet.

Ten days later, I was taken by ambulance to another hospital for rehabilitation. It was such joy to breathe the fresh air outside that hospital. The room in the new facility had a large window with a great view of San Francisco's rooftops. I felt joyous at discovering the world was still there and that I could walk forty feet with help. Five days later, just as I anticipated doing the four-minute mile, the doctor announced that my back was not healing well and that it must be infected. I was stunned and endured a bumpy, jolting ambulance ride back to UCSF Hospital for a second surgery.

Following two operations, I found myself having to get used to the metal structure in my back that resembled scaffolding, including cement, nails, and screws. During this period, I was compelled to draw on everything I knew about faith in God in order to survive. I had no choice but to surrender to His plan for me.

Music from a steel guitar brought me back to the restaurant and the present. The laughter around the table took over. I whispered, "Thank You, God. Grandma, you were so right." I am grateful for her ever-present advice to develop faith in God. Without that faith, I would not have made it. I would have given in to the voice that whispered—over and over again—*What are you doing here? This will never end,* the voice that made me feel alone and standing still and wondering if God would take my hand.

During rehab, holding on to my faith while struggling to maintain my sanity was the most difficult task I had ever encountered. I kept telling myself to be patient. Surely God would not bring me all this way—through my triumphs—to drop me now. I prayed so hard as I marked my calendar day by day—yearning to be free.

Now at last I was free of the hospital and laughing and talking loudly to be heard over the wonderful music. Grandma was right. God kept His promise to me, in His own time. Every time.

Faith in God is always borne out in the rewards we receive. Often the wait is unimaginable, and we cannot envision the depth and breadth of the outcome, but we have no choice but to wait on the Lord.

Melba Pattillo Beals is a recipient of this country's highest honor, the Congressional Gold Medal, for her role, as a fifteen-year-old, in the integration of Central High School in Little Rock, Arkansas. A retired university professor with a doctorate in International Multicultural Education, she is a former KQED television broadcaster, NBC television news reporter, ABC radio talk show host, and writer for various magazines, including *Family Circle* and *People*. Beals's *Warriors Don't Cry* has been in print for more than twenty years, has sold more than one million copies, and was the winner of the American Library Association Award, the Robert F. Kennedy Book Award, and the American Booksellers' Association Award. She lives in San Francisco and is the mother of three adult children.

Discover the courage, faith, and resolve of fourteen extraordinary women.

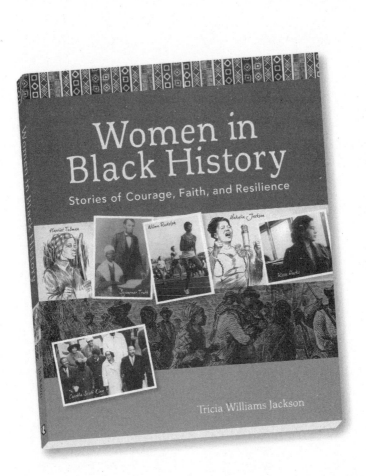

The Life, Legacy, and Lessons of a
CIVIL RIGHTS GIANT

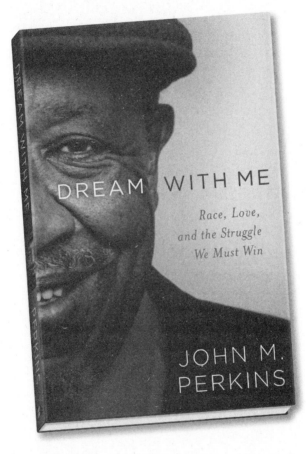

John M. Perkins has been there from the beginning. Raised by his grandmother, Perkins fled to California in 1947 after his brother was fatally shot by a town marshall. He led voter registration efforts and worked for school desegregation in the 1960s, and was imprisoned and tortured in 1970. Through it all, he has remained determined to seek justice and reconciliation based in Christ's redemptive work.